Whole-Hearted

FLOYD McCLUNG

WHOLE-HEARTED

LETTING JESUS
BE LORD

With Study Questions
for Individuals or Groups

Marshall Pickering
An Imprint of HarperCollinsPublishers

Marshall Pickering
An imprint of HarperCollins*Religious*,
Part of HarperCollins*Publishers*,
77–85 Fulham Palace Road
Hammersmith, London W6 8JB

The material in this book was adapted from four
volumes originally published by Marshall Pickering:
Effective Evangelism, *How to Have Victory Over Sin*,
Discovering Your Destiny and *Intimacy With God*. This
combined edition was first published in the United
States of America in 1990 by the InterVarsity Press
and in Great Britain in 1992 by Marshall Pickering

A catalogue record for this book is
available from the British Library

ISBN 0 551 02548 4

Printed in Great Britain by
HarperCollinsManufacturing Glasgow

To
Sally
who has
loved Jesus
with her whole
heart.

Contents

Acknowledgments

I wish to express my indebtedness and appreciation to Geoff and Janet Benge who helped write this book. Their names should really be on the cover. Geoff and Janet have been faithful friends and wonderful coauthors. Many of the ideas shared here came through the stimulation of conversations with them in meeting places as varied as Bozeman, Montana, and Amsterdam, Holland. Thank you, Geoff and Janet, for your friendship and for standing with me through the development of this book. I am very grateful.

Floyd McClung
Amsterdam, Holland

Have You Ever Felt Like a Failure?

I grew up feeling like a spiritual failure. When I was a teen-ager, we often had altar calls on Sunday nights at church which provided an opportunity for people to make a commitment to Jesus Christ. Time after time, my friends and I would go forward. We knew we were already saved, but somehow we still felt like failures. We were unable to keep all of the rules handed down to us. I remember the continual sense of condemnation. I was just never quite good enough. Yet my friends and I didn't want to go back to the world's way of doing things—we were stranded in no man's land! Why do so many of us, clinging to our faith, struggle on year after year but never seem to enjoy the victorious Christian life?

Since those early days as a Christian, I have discovered some biblical keys for experiencing this joy. These are keys that have liberated my personal walk with the Lord, and have brought freedom and release to many I have been privileged to talk with. They are simple things, but sometimes the simplest things are the most profound.

You'll find many of those keys in these pages. The first five chapters consider how we can actively bring every aspect of our lives into God's will. Knowing God's will involves much more than making a series of decisions that God would approve of. It means committing our entire lives to him as our sovereign Lord.

Chapters six through eight discuss ways we can remove from our lives the sin that so often pulls us away from God. Pride is such a core problem for so many that I have included two chapters on it (nine and ten), followed by a chapter on what has been considered to be the central Christian virtue and antidote to pride—humility.

The final chapters consider our responsibility in evangelism. The main reason Christ came as a man was to reconcile the world to himself. That is our primary duty as Christians as well. As our Lord, Christ is to be our model in character and action. Just as our whole lives are to be committed to Christ, so our whole lives speak the message of God's love for the world. Chapters twelve through fourteen emphasize that evangelism is not to be a sequence of isolated events in our lives, but the entirety of our lives.

Perhaps you feel you are not a "good" Christian. Perhaps you wonder how you could tell others of the grace of Jesus when you fail to experience that grace so often. Perhaps there is one sin that has defeated you for a long time. Regardless of your situation, God's Word promises victory. We can live in a close relationship with him.

Our attitude toward Jesus may sometimes be hardhearted or may sometimes be halfhearted. But with the power of his grace, our commitment to him can in fact be wholehearted.

One

Lord
of All

JESUS must be Lord of all of my life or he cannot be Lord at all. My *whole* life must be his. That does not mean that I must be perfect to accept Jesus Christ as my Savior. It does not mean that I must live the rest of my life sinlessly or that I won't struggle to give some things up to the Lord.

Most of us, for example, are emotionally attached to things such as food, friends, job or lifestyle. These give us feelings of security, identity and meaning. But as the Holy Spirit slowly penetrates our hearts, we realize our identity and security must be in the Lord.

Making Jesus Lord doesn't mean we will always follow him perfectly. It does mean that to the best of our knowledge we will submit everything in our lives to him and that we seek him, to the exclusion of all else, as our source of security. It also means that we will grow in the knowledge and understanding of what it means to make Jesus the Lord of our lives. Therefore, we should not be shocked that we need to continue to repent of things in life that are sinful. Making Jesus Lord means there is no intentional holding back.

Christ becomes, in effect, a benevolent despot. He, of course, is the only one in the universe qualified to hold that place in our hearts! It is because of his character and what he has done on the cross that he has earned the right to rule our lives so absolutely.

In my heart, and in every person's heart, there is a cross, and there is a throne. If I am seated upon the throne of my life, then, in effect, Jesus is dead in me. It means I have not invited him to come in his resurrection power to rule over me. If I get down off the throne, take up the cross (that is, "die" to my ambition and need to rule over my own life) and ask Jesus to take the throne and rule over my heart, then I have made Jesus the Lord of my life (Rom 8:9-17).

There are far too many professing Christians who want all the blessings of being a Christian—such as forgiveness, healing, hope and eternal life—but they do not want to pay the price of dying to their own will and letting Jesus rule over them. Jesus does not want to break our will, but he will cross it. We must subjugate our will to his. We must put his will above ours. In that process, we must die to ourselves in the sense that we will not insist on living for what we want first, but put his character and his desires above our own.

If we seek to bargain with God, the gospel will lose its effectiveness in our lives. There can be no compromise when it comes to making Jesus the Lord of our lives. He wants to be God over every dimension of our lives—friends, family, job, economic security, future plans, hobbies, recreation, lifestyle, living situations.

You might say, "Well, I'm doing pretty good. I have given most of those areas to the Lord, I am holding back on just one or two." I don't want to shock you, but that is not enough. Jesus does not want fifty-one per cent or even ninety-eight per cent control of our lives. He wants to be in control of all areas.

Picture your life like the chart below:

You might say, "I have given God everything except _____."
Is there one area that you have still held back from him? If so, you are telling God what part of your heart he can have. Even if you have given him control over most of your life, what you are really saying is that you are sitting on the throne of your heart, and you are telling God what part of your life is his! That will never do. If you are bargaining with God or trying to negotiate with him, then you have not yet comprehended what it means to be a real Christian. This may be why you do not have victory over sin.

Going Two Ways at Once

Not only is it an insult to the Creator of the universe to give him anything less than absolute control over our lives, but it is also insane. The most foolish thing a human can do is refuse the all-wise, loving, absolutely pure, holy, just, forgiving, merciful Creator of the universe and his rightful place over our lives as his creation.

Imagine Bill at a party. As he talks with his friend Mark, Mark says he'd like to take Bill out for a drink afterward. Since Bill had been saying that he would like to spend time with Mark, he accepts the invitation. "I will meet you outside after the party is over," Bill tells him.

A little while later, Jerry says to Bill, "I'd love to show you my new apartment."

Bill thinks, "I would love to see his new apartment, why not? I'll do it." So he says, "Yes, I will meet you outside the party and go with you."

After the party is over, he makes his way outside, and his two friends are waiting. Their cars are sitting side-by-side headed in opposite directions. Since Bill wants to go with both of them, he puts one foot inside one car and another foot inside the other car and says to both friends, "Let's go!"

Both friends take off at once and Bill finds himself in a very difficult situation! Psychologists have a term for this; they call it *frustration*. They define frustration as "having opposing goals."

People who try to live supremely both for themselves and for God, who try to go two different ways spiritually at the same time, will be frustrated people. There can be no victory in the Christian life if we are living for ourselves and trying to live for the Lord at the same time.

Again, I want to stress that this does not mean that our lives will be sinless or that we will live in some state of absolute perfection. What it means is that we submit to him to the best of our knowledge, and this knowledge will grow as God gives us more understanding through teaching and the study of his Word of what he expects and requires of us. As he does this, then at each new stage of life we must invite him afresh and anew to be our Lord. The relationship we have with the Lord should be dynamic and growing. His lordship is ever-expanding and increasing so that we know more and more what it means to invite him to rule over our lives.

Decisions, Decisions

Making Jesus Christ the Lord of all also means that we must put aside our selfish motives in decision making. There are at least three basic kinds of choices that every person makes.

1. Routine choices. These are the normal everyday decisions we make in business, family and school. These affect everything from what color clothes we should wear to what we eat to what newspapers we read.

2. Major choices. These are the choices that have much greater implications for our lives: Whom should I marry? Should I move to another city? What college should I go to? We don't make these decisions as often, and when we do make them, they have greater impact on us.

3. The ultimate choice. This choice can be made more than once, but it is only made about one thing. That is whether or not we will live for God.

It is possible to make routine and major choices for God, but on the ultimate level to continue to live for ourselves. We could picture that in the following way:

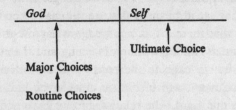

"Making choices for self, rather than God."

We can make decisions to go to church, to be church members, to give money, to sing in the choir or to do other wonderful and important things for God; however, if our ultimate motives are to do them for self-gratification, to impress other people or to do these for selfish motives, then what we have is a well-refined state of hypocrisy.

The result is merely good works. It is possible for us to call ourselves Christians, do good things for Jesus and die and go to hell. The Bible says in Matthew 7:21, "Not everyone who says to me, 'Lord, Lord' shall enter the kingdom of heaven, but he who does the will of my Father who is in heaven." That is why it is so important to make Jesus our Lord from a motive to please him and not to get something from him. We must give him our businesses, our families and our relationships to bring joy to his heart.

The motivation for making Jesus the Lord of our lives should not be to get ourselves into heaven, to impress God with our spirituality or to try to get God to love us. Jesus wants us to choose him as Lord because we understand who he is, what he has done for us on the cross and how we can never live our lives without him. He wants us to make this choice out of a selfless motive of pleasing him and not only for what we can get from it.

As you have read through this chapter, has it become apparent to you that there are things that you have held back from the Lord Jesus? Are there dimensions of your life that you have not put under his lordship? Perhaps you have even come to the startling discovery, which some professing Christians do, that all their life they have been doing their religious good deeds but their motivation has been overwhelmingly selfish.

If you have made that kind of discovery, there is only one adequate response. I encourage you to bow before the Lord Jesus, confess your need of him, ask him to forgive you for your selfishness and choose to make him the Lord of your life. Receive by faith the forgiveness of your sins (1 Jn 1:6-9).

You may want to take time to think through what this means. When you do make the choice, please do so knowing that the Lord Jesus loves you deeply and only wants to do what is best for your life. His desire to rule over your life is motivated by his love for you and his commitment to share a relationship with you that liberates you to be all he created you to be.

When we put Jesus first in our lives, we unleash the power of the Creator of the universe to dwell within us. The resurrected, infinite, all-powerful Creator comes to live inside of us! And in his coming to dwell within us he promises to give us ultimate victory over sin!

It is no small thing to invite Jesus to be your Savior and Lord. You and I, as creatures, are acknowledging that we are made by the Creator. When this happens, not only are we committing ourselves to him, but he is committing himself to us. In making that commitment, he says, "I will guarantee your ultimate victory. I will watch over you and go with you. As long as you will submit to me, I will ensure your victory over sin and your eternal fellowship with me."

The Scope of Victory
The greatest motivation to victory in the Christian life is this assurance that Jesus is within us and his grace is greater than any temptation we will ever face. He is more committed to our victory over sin than we are! As it says in Romans 8:31-39:

> If God is for us, who can be against us? He who did not spare his own Son, but gave him up for us all—how will he not also, along with him, graciously give us all things? Who will bring any charge against those whom God has chosen? It is God who justifies. Who is he that condemns? Christ Jesus, who died—more than that, who was raised to life—is at the right hand of God and is also interceding for us. Who shall separate us from the love of Christ? Shall trouble or hardship or persecution or famine or nakedness or danger or sword? As it is written: "For your sake we face death all day long; we are considered as sheep to be slaughtered." No, in all these we are more than conquerors through him who loved us. For I am convinced that neither death nor life, neither angels nor demons, neither the present nor the future, nor any powers, neither height nor depth, nor anything else in all creation, will be able to separate us from the love of God that is in Christ Jesus our Lord.

I can remember talking with Corrie ten Boom about this passage of Scripture. She looked at me and said, "Floyd, the phrase 'in all these things' means just what it says. That is the scope of our victory." I was deeply moved when I understood that God promises us that we will be more than conquerors in everything we face in life. Everything means *everything*. That is his promise to us.

What is the source of this victory? It is "through him who loved us." We are not talking about some kind of a self-power, positive thinking, pull-yourself-up-by-your-bootstraps kind of Christianity. What we are saying here is that Jesus Christ is the source of our victory over sin. He promises us that we will not only be victorious, but more than victorious.

That does not mean that we will not face problems. In fact, it says *in* all these things, not above these things or outside of these things. In other words, we will face tribulation, distress, persecution, stress, peril, sword, death, principalities and powers. But, as we yield our lives to the lordship of Christ, then he will give us the victory.

It also says in Ephesians 1:4: "For he chose us in him before the creation of the world to be holy and blameless in his sight." This is God's will for us! He wants us to conquer sin. Therefore, if we will submit to God, he, by his Spirit, will come and help us do what is his will for us.

Paul goes on to say in Ephesians 1:7-8, "In him we have redemption through his blood, the forgiveness of sins, in accordance with the riches of God's grace that he lavished on us." A little later, he says that God has called us to a hope and a glorious inheritance that includes God's great power and the privilege to be in Christ, as he rules over authorities, powers and dominions. If we will abide in Christ—that is, if we totally submit our life to him to the best of our knowledge—then God will raise us up together with Christ and give us the power to conquer sin.

I encourage you, if you struggle with this, to read through Ephesians 1:1-23 and pray each verse out loud. Personalize each verse. Get on your knees, open the Bible and speak those words as promises made to you. Say to the Lord: "Lord, I claim your promise in Ephesians 1:5-7 that you have predestined us in love to be your children through Jesus Christ according to the purpose of your will. And that you have redeemed me through your blood and given me the forgiveness of my trespasses according to the riches of your grace which you have lavished upon me."

Making the Scripture personal in this way will help make it real to you. Sometimes it is easy to get in the trap of feeling God is trying to push us down and that Christianity is just a list of don'ts. When you read the words of Paul in Ephesians 1, it is clear that God is not against us but for us. He created us and he loves us. He wants the best for us. We need to respond to his love by making Jesus the Lord over all of our life. Receiving Christ as Lord assures us of our victory. Not because of our choice to make him Lord, but because he truly is Lord!

Pride can be a major obstacle to our making Jesus Lord and experiencing true repentance. Instead of receiving God's grace freely, it's easy to slip into a pattern of earning that grace. We begin to say things like, "When I get to the stage of praying for three hours a day, I'll really feel like a good Christian." But God is not waiting for us to come up to a certain standard before he will love us and help us. He wants us just as we are! He may want us to pray more than we do, but he wants us to start where we are, and not think that by doing more for him he will love us more.

An Impossible Debt

This point is nowhere more clearly illustrated than a situation which occurred in a church in California several years ago. With the influx of Vietnamese refugees into the United States, the church decided to sponsor a number of families. Asians, though, have a very different system of values than do Westerners, so some misunderstandings occurred. One of these was in trying to get the refugees to feel they were under no obligation to the church. Some of them felt such a burden of obligation toward their sponsors that they did not even want to see them.

To those not familiar with Asian culture, this was interpreted as ungratefulness. The truth, however, was that the refugees realized there was no way they could ever repay the sponsors and so were too embarrassed to face them. Some went as far as moving out of the area. How tragic this was. All the sponsors had wanted was to see the refugees happily resettled, instead of striving to repay an impossible debt. They had sponsored them out of love to bring them freedom, not make them feel indebted.

I think God often feels like those sponsors when we try and earn the grace and freedom he wants to give us. We can't earn his grace. He wants us to freely accept and appropriate it in our life so that we can daily enjoy Christian living. As we do that, we are receiving the grace and power of Almighty God to overcome sin in our lives. We are receiving the ultimate and certain victory that is ours through Jesus Christ and his death and resurrection.

Questions for Individuals or Groups

1. What does it mean to you for Jesus to be Lord of your life?

2. How do you feel when you read, "Jesus does not want fifty-one per cent or even ninety-eight per cent control of our lives. He wants to be in control of all areas" (p. 13)?

3. Why is holding back part of our lives from Christ similar to Bill trying to leave a party with two different friends at the same time (pp. 14)?

4. Why is motive so important in a decision to make Christ the Lord of our lives (pp. 16-17)?

5. Why does God want us to put our lives completely under his control?

6. As you consider aspects of your life that you have trouble submitting to Christ, what can motivate you and empower you to give everything to him (pp. 18-21)?

7. What is your response to the story at the end of the chapter about the impossible debt?

8. What light does it shed for you on the issue of Christ's lordship?

9. How can we submit every aspect of our lives to Christ—friends, family, job, finances, plans, hobbies, recreation, lifestyle and so on?

Two

The Framework
of Obedience

ONCE we give our lives to God, the first question is often "What does he want me to do with my life?" Many Christians focus this question on issues of career and marriage. But God has much more in mind than this. And what he has in mind is not hard to discover.

Scripture reveals certain principles and truths that are God's will for us regardless of our personal situations and circumstances. Obedience to God in the ten areas which I discuss in the following pages is the prerequisite for knowing more of his will. To know God's will for the future, we must first obey what we already know in the present!

As we look more closely at what God's Word says about his purpose for our lives, let me suggest that you take a notebook and write the verse for each area at the top of a page. Prayer-fully ask God to show you whether you are at present fulfilling his will in this area of your life. Refer back to your notebook on a regular basis and ask, "Am I closer to God in this area now than I was six months ago?"

Believing in Christ

It is God's will that we believe in the Lord Jesus. "And this is his command: to believe in the name of his Son, Jesus Christ" (1 Jn 3:23). Belief in God and faith in his Son Jesus Christ is the most fundamental truth of the Bible, and without it we can never be Christians. Indeed, Christians in the early church were known as "believers." They heard of the things Jesus said and did, they read the letters the apostles and other eyewitnesses wrote, and they believed.

The Philippian jailer asked, "What must I do to be saved?" Paul's answer was refreshingly simple, "Believe in the Lord Jesus, and you will be saved" (Acts 16:30-31). We must never forget that trust in the Lord Jesus is the cornerstone of our Christian faith and is therefore God's will for our lives. He wants a relationship with each one of us, and that is why he sent his Son into the world.

Surrendering Yourself

It is God's will that we give ourselves one hundred per cent to him. "Therefore, I urge you, brothers, in view of God's mercy, to offer your bodies as living sacrifices, holy and pleasing to God—this is your spiritual act of worship" (Rom 12:1).

Many people want to know God's will to decide whether or not they will obey it! They have the attitude, "Give me plenty of warning God; explain all of the details, and I'll decide and get in touch with you if I'm available."

God, however, expects unconditional surrender from us. The fact that Almighty God asks for our surrender should be enough to totally guarantee it! We are not two equals locked in debate; only pride can fool us into that delusion.

We are finite; God is infinite. We are fallible; he is infallible. We waver; he is constant. We are the created; he is the Creator. He is without fault; we are sinners. He asks us to submit ourselves to his will because of who he is. He is the only wise God, and he knows what is best for us in every situation.

God's purposes for humankind are always benevolent and merciful. He is for us, not against us (Rom 8:28-32). He longs to save and redeem people, and wants to see each of us reach our full potential. Because of his wonderful character, we can trust him and have complete confidence in his character and his purpose for our lives.

What God wants to hear from us is: "Anything, anytime, anywhere. I trust you, Lord. You speak and I will obey." Only when he hears this can he truly guide our lives with specific directions.

Loving the Lost

It is God's will that we love the lost. "The Lord is not slow in keeping his promise, as some understand slowness. He is patient with you, not wanting anyone to perish, but everyone to come to repentance" (2 Pet 3:9).

God yearns for people to hear the gospel and be saved. What are we doing to see his will fulfilled in this area? Sharing the gospel is not the responsibility of a handful of "professionals," it is the responsibility of all Christians.

There are those who have no difficulty sharing the gospel. They have an outgoing personality that enables them to preach on street corners, pray at their office desk or pass out tracts to strangers in the subway. However, many of us are not that bold, yet we still have a responsibility to share his love with others.

God made each of us the way we are. He gave us our personalities, and we must find ways to share the gospel that are consistent with whom he made us to be. We may never stand and preach on a street corner, but we could pray for the person who does. We may be uncomfortable handing out tracts, but we could volunteer to fold those tracts for the person who hands them out. In fact, we may never have anything to do with tracts and street meetings. God may want us to talk with business associates. We could share a Christian record or magazine with a friend, or we could try to meet a specific need we know they have. There are hundreds of creative and effective ways of evangelizing, and we must allow God to show us ways that are effective for us.

Youth With A Mission, the mission agency I work with, has a strong emphasis on evangelism, but by no means are we all born evangelists. However, each person in the mission is furthering the cause of the gospel. Some make dinner for drama teams. Others write brochures to encourage people to participate in overseas outreaches. Still others prepare financial records and oversee day-to-day logistical operations. Our mission would be in total disarray if it were not for these people.

The same is true within the context of the local church. Not everyone can or wants to be at the front preaching or leading a Sunday-school class. Yet, all have their parts to play. Perhaps there are children in the neighborhood who would like to attend Sunday school if someone encouraged them and provided rides on Sunday mornings. The pastor cannot personally invite everyone in the area to attend church, but the combined effort of those in the church could mean an influx of potential converts.

Each of us needs to pray and ask God for opportunities to do his will in the area of evangelism. I'll have a lot more to say about this in chapters twelve, thirteen and fourteen. In the meantime, don't be deterred. You can, and must, make a difference!

Doing Good Works

It is God's will that we do good works in Christ. "We are God's workmanship, created in Christ Jesus to do good works, which God prepared in advance for us to do" (Eph 2:10).

James tells us faith without works is dead. Faith is the inward part of our Christian life, the part no one can see. Good works, on the other hand, are the outward part. Everyone can see our good works, or lack of them, but they cannot see the state of our faith.

Faith is like the roots of a tree. Works are the fruit. We don't judge how healthy a tree is by digging it up and inspecting its roots. Instead, we examine its fruit. If there is no fruit, we assume the roots to be diseased or dying. Likewise, if there are no good works visible in our lives as Christians, then our faith is in bad shape. If this is the case, it is imperative that we examine our faith and correct that problem so our faith won't die altogether.

Are we doing good works in the situation God has placed us in? They don't need to be spectacular. They can be simple things like babysitting a friend's children or helping a neighbor get his or her car started on a cold morning. Seek out opportunities to serve others. If the prospect of doing good works doesn't excite you, then you need to expose your roots of faith to the Holy Spirit and have him tend them.

Growing in Faith

It is God's will that we grow spiritually. "Make every effort to supplement your faith with virtue, and virtue with knowledge, and knowledge with self-control, and self-control with stead-fastness, and steadfastness with godliness, and godliness with brotherly affection, and brotherly affection with love" (2 Pet 1:5-7 RSV).

Some extremes in theological thinking suggest we ask the Lord into our lives and then sit back and wait for him to take us to heaven. These verses certainly do not confirm that view. We are to make every effort to increase our faith, knowledge, self-control, steadfastness and brotherly affection. Each of us is expected to be spiritually self-sustaining. We cannot rely on pastors or Christian leaders to keep our faith propped up.

Some Christians live from Sunday to Sunday. They start their week ready for action, but by Saturday are drained of their enthusiasm and can barely drag themselves to church the next day for another boost. Paul talks of digesting the milk of the Word (1 Cor 3:2). Babies need someone to feed them milk, and in the same way, new Christians need someone to help them understand biblical truth. Yet, we have all seen retarded adults who are incapable of feeding themselves. Behavior that is natural and cute in an infant is saddening to watch in these adults. Sadly, there are Christians who have not made "every effort to supplement their faith," and they too are retarded in their spiritual development.

Prayer and Bible study are important in supplementing our faith. God reveals himself to us in the Bible, and through prayer we have direct access to him with our problems and questions. There are many good books that can help us establish a personal prayer life. We need to read them and learn from them so that through prayer we can spiritually sustain ourselves.

Likewise, there are many good Bible study guides that we can follow. Some go through the Bible book by book, others topic by topic. Try the different approaches and see which is the most rewarding for you, then stick with it. Once Bible study is a regular part of our lives, we will begin to reap the rewards of a more stable and mature relationship with the Lord. We will also have the personal confidence to go to the Bible and find our own answers to life's questions.

God does not want us to be spiritually retarded and unable to sustain the new life he has given us. He wants us to reach a place of maturity where we can spiritually feed ourselves and be able to stand firm in the face of any adversity.

Submitting to Authority

It is God's will that we submit to governing authorities. "Submit yourselves for the Lord's sake to every authority instituted among men: whether to the king, as the supreme authority, or to governors, who are sent by him to punish those who do wrong and to commend those who do right. For it is God's will that by doing good you should silence the ignorant talk of foolish men" (1 Pet 2:13-15).

I remember riding in a car along a Los Angeles freeway with

a driver I didn't know very well. Before long he had the accelerator pedal down to the floor. As we sped along, he glanced at me and explained apologetically that he had a "demon of speed." Not long afterward a police car pulled in behind us. Miraculously, he brought his demon under instant control! "It" was perfectly well-behaved until the police car turned off at an exit, then suddenly it flared up again! While this story has a funny side, it is also serious. We honor God by obeying those over us, even on the freeway.

As long as the governing authorities are honest and unselfish, most of us can submit to them. But what about submitting to human laws that contradict the laws of God? At that point we must put God's laws above civil law. Absolute obedience is only given to God. Governments are ordained by God for the good of humanity, and when they exploit and abuse their responsibilities and the people they govern, they must be held accountable both to God and to the people they serve.

Obedience to the laws of God may lead us to disobey human laws—or to be in conflict with what we are asked to do by the rulers over us. We must be prepared as Christians to resist unrighteousness, corruption, prejudice, immorality, oppression and every other form of evil. We should do that with love in our hearts, for the gospel is so radical that it commands us to love our enemies (Lk 6:32-36). That is what makes Christianity so powerful—we can submissively disobey, lovingly resist, passionately and intensely refuse to give in to evil people and corrupt systems, while we forgive those who are sinning against us.

Enduring Hardship
God wants us to be ready and willing to suffer for the gospel.

"Consider it pure joy, my brothers, whenever you face trials of many kinds, because you know that the testing of your faith develops perseverance. Perseverance must finish its work so that you may be mature and complete, not lacking anything" (Jas 1:2-4).

When faced with difficulties, it is easy to question whether we really are in the will of God. But it is entirely possible to be in the will of God and still endure difficulties. Throughout our Christian lives, God will use difficult situations as a way of developing our characters, and we can never become mature Christians without them. There is no armchair correspondence course for becoming a mature Christian—we must all go through struggles to get there. So, we must learn to embrace difficulties and trials as opportunities for developing spiritual muscle. We need these times and should not shy away from them. Don't pray for an easy life. Pray for the strength to become a steadfast Christian.

Denying Yourself

It is God's will that we follow his Spirit rather than our selfish desires. "So as to live the rest of the time in the flesh no longer for the lusts of men, but for the will of God" (1 Pet 4:2 NASB).

In life, we must choose to go in one of two directions. One is the way of human lusts. The other is doing the will of God. The two are complete opposites. At one end of the scale we go our own way and enjoy what we consider to be the pleasures of life. At the other end, we submit to the will of God and live our lives to please him.

The word *lust* is used today mainly in relation to sex, but its meaning is much broader than that. To lust is to passionately or overwhelmingly desire something. We can lust for a higher-paying job, a new car, stereo or any physical thing. We can even lust to "get even" with another person. Living life in this way is living according to the lusts of the flesh.

Jesus tells us that unless we deny ourselves, take up the cross and live for him, we are not fit for his kingdom. This may seem harsh and uncompromising, but given this world's condition, it is the only alternative we have. If we choose to ignore Jesus and continue living to fulfill the lusts of the flesh, our lives will be marked by confusion, disappointment, heartache and, ultimately, destruction.

Most non-Christians are accustomed to living freely by their feelings. If they desire something, they go after it. As Christians we are taught in the Bible to make our choices based on truth, not on what feels good. When a person first becomes a Christian there can be a tremendous inner conflict between these two ways of living. If we are accustomed to living by our feelings, we will not "feel good" about the Christian life, but if we persist in putting truth above pleasure, after a time we will find our pleasure from truth!

Doing Justice

It is God's will that we defend the rights of the poor. "Let us consider how we may spur one another on toward love and good deeds. Let us not give up meeting together, as some are in the habit of doing, but let us encourage one another—and all the more as you see the Day approaching" (Heb 10:24-25).

It is God's will for us to do justice and to love mercy. "He has showed you, O man, what is good. And what does the

LORD require of you? To act justly and to love mercy, and to walk humbly with your God" (Mic 6:8).

We live in a world that is filled with injustice and inequality. As Christians, God calls us to make sure nothing we do contributes to the exploitation of those who are defenseless and poor (Amos 1:27; 5:1-6). In fact, we are commanded to defend the rights of the poor (Ps 82:3). Because they are defenseless, we are to defend them (Prov 31:9). This will mean that at times there will, of necessity, be confrontation with those who oppress the poor. It is inevitable if we are defending those who are the victims of greed or oppression.

Because poverty creates hopelessness and lack of power over one's own life, a certain listlessness and apathy can result in the poor. Thus, it is dangerous to judge people quickly when they appear to be lazy. Perhaps they are suffering from the results of lack of motivation, ignorance, despair or bad parenting. Helping people out of such poverty requires great patience and mercy. That is one reason why the Lord commands us to love mercy.

Further, doing justice and loving mercy does not mean we have all the answers. A paternalistic attitude toward the poor says as much about our needs as the needs of others. We have much to learn from all people. If we are to serve others we must not decide what their problems are and then impose our solutions. We are to serve all people from a basis of a solid relationship. If we are not willing to take time to develop genuine friendships with the oppressed and poor in society, we should not try to get involved in their lives. We could do more harm than good.

Forgiving Others

It is God's will for us to love and forgive those who offend us.

Scripture exhorts us to do so:

> My prayer is . . . that all of them may be one, Father, just as you are in me and I am in you. May they also be in us so that the world may believe that you have sent me. I have given them the glory that you gave me, that they may be one as we are one: I in them and you in me. May they be brought to complete unity to let the world know that you sent me and have loved them even as you have loved me. (Jn 17:20-23)

> Be completely humble and gentle; be patient, bearing with one another in love. (Eph 4:2)

> Be kind and compassionate to one another, forgiving each other, just as in Christ God forgave you. (Eph 4:32)

There is probably no area of life where it is more difficult to obey biblical truth than in broken and difficult relationships. We are taught in the Bible to love our enemies and pray for those who persecute us (Lk 6:32-36; Mt 5:46). If we are offended by someone, it is God's will for us to forgive them. If forgiveness is difficult, we must keep on forgiving until we are healed of the bitterness and freely forgive them. We must choose to love the offending person with God's love as an act of obedience and faith.

Some relationships come easy. Others have to be worked at. Love and unity do not happen by accident. It is a result of making the right choices over and over again. God does not expect us to continue endlessly in a destructive relationship that is physically or emotionally damaging. But even if we withdraw from a person because it is too painful, God still wants us to forgive them. By forgiving, we release bitterness from our lives and rise above the other person's faults and weaknesses (Prov 15:17-18; 14:7). As we love and forgive one another, God's love is released into our lives, and it becomes a powerful witness to the reality of his presence.

The preceding ten principles are the will of God for each of us. Before God can use us or give us "special assignments," he has to know if we can be trusted with what he has already given us. If we want to be used by God and enter into the destiny he has for us, we must first take care of these basics.

Questions for Individuals or Groups

1. Why are you interested in knowing God's will?

2. God has already revealed a great deal of his will for us in the Bible. The author says that obedience to his already revealed will is a prerequisite for knowing more of his will (p. 35). Do you agree or disagree? Explain.

3. What do good works tell us about someone's faith (p. 27)?

4. What does it mean to you to grow spiritually (pp. 28-29)?

5. The author says that at times it may be God's will for us to disobey government authorities in order to obey God (p. 30). Do you agree or disagree? Explain.

If you agree, in what particular circumstances might it be appropriate to break the law?

6. When, according to McClung, can it be God's will for us to suffer (p. 31)?

Do you think this means Christians are supposed to have long faces and never enjoy themselves? Explain.

7. Helping the poor is another major concern God has. What have been your experiences with helping the homeless or defenseless?

What opportunities exist for you to be involved with the poor?

8. Finally, the author mentions forgiveness. Why is healing broken relationships often so difficult?

What can you do to be reconciled to someone you might have hard feelings toward?

Three

Being Faithful

RECENTLY a pastor in the Midwest relayed the following problem to one of our mission leaders:

We have a young couple who came home from Youth With A Mission to raise financial support. They asked if the church would consider supporting them, and in return they would commit themselves to the church for one year. We agreed to this arrangement. But, for the six months they've been with us we only see them once a week—Sunday mornings. They don't offer to take Sunday school, take turns cleaning or help with the youth group. If that's their idea of serving, then we feel used and don't think they have what it takes to be a missionary. We don't want to support them because they're not worth sending out as missionaries with your organization.

When I heard of the situation, I thought: "The pastor is right. This couple does not deserve to be supported or to be full-time missionaries. They haven't been responsible. They haven't shown humility and proved themselves in the local church."

To deal with the problem one of our leaders visited the couple. He pointed out to them the situation in which they had put the church missions board. He also visited the pastor, who was very gracious and agreed to give the couple a second chance. The story had a happy ending. The couple stayed on at the church helping wherever they could. Eventually they were commissioned and sent out with the church's financial backing and blessing.

If we cannot serve God in the situation we're in right now, then what makes us think we can do better in a different location or position? The human tendency is to avoid the mundane and graduate to the spectacular, but that is not God's way. Godly character exemplified through the fruit of the Spirit can be as easily seen in small tasks as it can in large ones.

The best way to find out how we can serve God most effectively is by serving him where we are. Many of us have met people who claim they are called to do great things for God. However, while they're waiting for "great things" to start happening, they do nothing. They are unwilling to do anything "less" than their "calling." But that is not God's way; he wants us to start out by being faithful where we are.

Throughout the Bible, God gives to people promises of the great things he wants to do through them, but seldom are the promises fulfilled immediately. There are often aspects of their character that have to be worked out before they are ready to handle the ministry or opportunity God has for them.

If, for instance, you feel called to work with children, then start where the need is. Arrive an hour before Sunday school and make sure the classrooms are clean and the chairs are set out. Stack the chairs and sweep the floor afterward. Be early for the Monday-night prayer meeting and any other relevant church activity during the week. By doing this you will take the first steps toward knowing God's will—*being an available servant.*

God wants to start training us for the future—*now.* He wants to develop in us the character strengths of stability, consistency and responsibility. These are traits most easily and efficiently developed in the local church. We do not become effective missionaries simply by crossing the sea.

Though God gives us promises and gifts to inspire us, there is a process of preparation we must go through. Jesus speaks about this in Luke 16:10-12. In these verses he clarifies three areas of character training that are essential for every true disciple. Take time and pray over the following three areas of faithfulness as preparation for doing more for the Lord.

1. Faithful with Little

If we are faithful in the little things God gives us to do now, his word says we will also be "faithful in much." In Matthew 25 Jesus tells a parable about faithfulness. A master gave each of his servants varying amounts of money before leaving on a long trip. They did not all receive the same amount of money, in much the same way as we all have differing levels of skill and ability.

Upon his return the master inquired as to what his servants had done with the money he'd given them. He discovered that the first two servants had invested the money wisely and now had twice as much. The third, however, had buried his money and had only the amount the master had given him.

Jesus drew an interesting conclusion from this, "For everyone who has will be given more, and he will have an abundance. Whoever does not have, even what he has will be taken from him" (Mt 25:29). Though this passage speaks of wise stewardship over money, the principle applies to every area of life.

Some have thought that if they only had a new car they'd look after it better than their present one. However, when they get the new car, it doesn't take long before they treat it the same as they treated the old car. Why? Because they did not prove themselves with what they already had. If they had disciplined themselves into taking care of the old car, they would have no problem taking care of their new one.

Similarly, many people believe in giving to God's work, but don't because they think they don't have enough money to start. But the same principle applies—prove yourself with what you have and God will entrust you with more. If we wait until we have "enough" money, we may never begin. We must learn to be faithful with what God has already given us.

2. Faithful with Physical Things

If we are to be used by God in serving others, we must learn to be faithful in the "little things" in life. Through our diligence and reliability, we demonstrate to God and others that we can be counted on. We show that we are serious about serving God.

The word that is used for physical things in Luke 16 is *mammon*. What is mammon? Mammon translated means "riches" and, more particularly, "all the material things that riches can buy." Are we faithful over the things we are given responsibility for? Some believe "earthly things" are not important to the kingdom of God. In many ways, though, handling money is a Christian's apprenticeship to higher things. Therefore, we must carefully handle our material possessions.

"Whoever can be trusted with very little can also be trusted with much, and whoever is dishonest with little will also be dishonest with much. So, if you have not been trustworthy in handling worldly wealth, who will trust you with true riches?" (Lk 16:10-11). Jesus tells us we must prove ourselves with physical things before we can be trusted with spiritual gifts. If we prove to be faithful with mammon, we can then be entrusted with spiritual responsibility.

Do we pay our bills on time, and are we scrupulously honest with our taxes? Do we take care of maintenance on our homes and cars? Are we faithful in the tasks assigned to us at work? These life situations are God's test to see if we are ready for greater responsibility and trust in his kingdom. How we handle mammon does affect the way God can use us in his kingdom.

3. Faithful in Other People's Ministries

"And if you have not been faithful in that which is another's property, who will give you that which is your own?" (Lk 16:12 RSV).

It's easy to get spiritual when considering the will of God, but this verse puts things on a very practical level. Are we faithful with possessions that belong to other people? Do we borrow things and not return them? Are we more careless with others' possessions than we are with our own? Do we give our employers our best, or are we lax on the job, leaving early when they are not around? Do we follow instructions to the best of our ability, or are we always trying to do things our way? If we are not faithful in these areas, why do we suppose God will give us bigger tasks and more authority?

The most prominent pastors and spiritual leaders around the world today did not start out with high-profile ministries. They began by working under others and serving their vision. They proved themselves; they demonstrated they could be trusted to undertake and complete a task. As they did this, over time, they were recognized and given more authority. I believe this is the biblical model: Prove yourself capable of tending another person's "vineyard." Serve the vision and calling of another, and God will give you your own, not as a reward, but because you have learned to put others above yourself.

The life of Joseph provides a picture of this principle at work. Through a dream, God gave Joseph a promise that his brothers would serve him. However, Joseph had much character development in store before he was ready for the fulfillment of that promise.

Eventually he found himself in an Egyptian jail where, I'm sure, he spent a lot of time wondering what had gone wrong. During this time in jail, God tested and prepared Joseph, and when he had proved himself faithful he was given a greater task with great authority. (Notice that Joseph ended up doing on a large scale exactly what he had proven himself faithful in doing while in jail: overseeing people and resources.) Through his faithfulness, he proved he was ready for the fulfillment of the promise, and his brothers did bow before him and serve him (Gen 37—47).

Waiting for God

God also made promises to King Saul, Israel's first king. We often cast Saul as the "bad guy," forgetting he was given his position by God. The problem for Saul was that his character could not sustain the authority God entrusted to him. Despite repeated opportunities to prove himself, he failed, and God was eventually forced to remove the power, authority and blessing he had bestowed upon Saul and give it instead to David.

Many think that once they get a position they'll rise to the occasion, and do and be everything God requires of them. The story of Saul, however, illustrates that this is not true. Position and authority may only compound areas of weakness in our character, and we would be better off dealing with them before we pursue any ministry. To do so will save much heartache and embarrassment.

Unlike Saul, David knew God had called him to be king, but did not seek the kingship. Instead, he trusted God to bring it about. On several occasions David had an opportunity to kill Saul and claim the position God had promised, but he did not. He wanted to receive it in God's way and in God's time, and eventually his patience and faithfulness were rewarded.

God's promises to us are never an excuse to ride over others in pursuit of God's will. God will fulfill his word to us in due time. Testing and proving come first, and we dare not attempt to shortcut them. God wants to hear each of us say, "I'll do this your way. It's your promise, and I trust you to bring it about."

What happens if I know God has called me to be a missionary but my spouse is not interested or I have obligations to family? What do I do? Do I give up on what God has promised?

God wants us to be faithful even if what we can do seems so little in comparison to the things we could do were our circumstances more favorable. Perhaps there's a nearby community of the same ethnic group God has called us to. We could attend church there and get involved in outreach and visitation, or we could enroll in a language school and learn their language. As God sees us being faithful, he builds our character, and when we finally get where God has called us, we will be so much better prepared.

Ten years ago Mark felt God call him to minister in China. At that time it was very difficult for a Westerner to go to China, even as a tourist, let alone as a missionary. Nevertheless, Mark trusted God and began looking for practical ways in which he could prepare himself.

He went to the library, borrowed Mandarin-language tapes and began learning the language. He read all the books the library had on life in China. About five or six years later, when the doors to China began to open, Mark was there, equipped and ready. He applied to the Chinese government for a job teaching English as a second language, for which he was accepted and sent to a remote province.

Mark is still in China today. He has free access to the student dormitories where he holds evening Bible studies. As a result of his efforts he has been able to lead many of his student friends to a relationship with Jesus Christ. Had Mark been unfaithful and failed to take the initiative when God spoke to him he would not be doing what he is doing in China today.

Faithfulness is like the hinge on a door. It is only a small thing yet without it even the largest of doors will not open. By being faithful in everything God has presently spoken to us, we make a hinge on which he can swing the door wide open for us in the future.

Questions for Individuals or Groups

1. What kind of ministry do you think God has called you to?

2. What kinds of responsibilities do you have now?

3. How can faithfulness now in these responsibilities prepare you for ministry in the future?

4. The author points out that God wants us to be faithful in small ways before he gives us larger tasks (pp. 39-40). Why do you think it is often hard to consistently do small jobs well?

5. Next McClung suggests that how we handle mammon is an indication of how we will handle spiritual responsibilities (pp. 40-41). How would you evaluate your responsibility with finances? With your possessions?

6. The third area of faithfulness noted is taking care of what belongs to others. The author asks, "Do we borrow things and not return them? Are we more careless with others' possessions than we are with our own? Do we give our employers our best, or are we lax on the job?" (p. 41). Can you freely serve the ministry and vision God has given to others? What answers would you give to these questions?

7. Often we can't move right away into the ministry that we want from God or that we think he is calling us to. What practical steps can you take now to prepare for when the time is right?

Four

Be All God Wants You to Be

GOD has made us to live for his glory. And he has made us individually and uniquely. He's given us each special abilities, circumstances and backgrounds. That means that if we want to follow Jesus as our Lord, we will sometimes have a very particular set of questions to bring before him: Should I take a job or go to school? Should I travel or stay home? Should I get married or not? Should I teach Sunday school or help at the soup kitchen? Should I make this investment or another? The answers to many of these sorts of questions are not usually found explicitly in the Bible.

We all want to know the answer to the question "Lord, what do you want me to do?" The last two chapters form the basis upon which we can have confidence to step out in faith and follow God. When we are wholehearted for him, we can have the faith we need to ask God specific questions about our lives. There are, however, some general principles that can help us answer the kinds of questions mentioned above. This chapter will consider how our God-given personalities, preferences and aptitudes can begin to do that. The next chapter looks at more specific issues.

Knowing Your Talents

There is a segment of the body of Christ which has what I call "the martyr complex." These Christians automatically know God is going to force them to do the very thing they hate most. If they like warm weather, God will obviously call them to Alaska, or, if they like working with gadgets and machines, they're destined to spend the rest of their lives on a remote Pacific island where there are no electric sockets.

We must be very careful with this kind of attitude lest we misrepresent God's character and portray him as a gigantic kill-joy. There may be times when God requires us to do something we do not enjoy and would not naturally choose, but since God created us to be the kind of people we are. He pays careful attention to our personalities and natural gifts when he gives us special assignments.

What are our spiritual gifts? And what special assignment does God have for us? Many find it hard to answer these questions because it is difficult to get a balanced and objective view of ourselves. Sometimes we think we're better at something than we really are, or conversely, we fail to recognize our strengths and abilities.

We all know people who have unrealistic estimations of their abilities and gifts. We've heard of the choir member with the worst voice singing with the most gusto, the person who has no rapport with children volunteering to run the Sunday school, much to the chagrin of the children. Why, we wonder, can't they see their lack of talent for the job?

When evaluating themselves, people tend to swing toward one of two extremes. They either underestimate or overestimate their abilities, and both are debilitating. We are admonished in Scripture not to think more highly of ourselves than we ought. Yet, today there are many Christians sitting in pews doing nothing because they feel they haven't been offered a position that is worthy of them. They have an overestimation of their abilities. In waiting to be recognized, they are in grave danger of missing God's opportunity for them.

Conversely, we should not think less of ourselves than we ought. Many people are waiting in the wings until they feel more worthy or until they have something spiritual to offer. However, spiritual gifts and natural abilities are both discovered and developed by stepping out and doing something that needs to be done.

It is not a sign of spirituality to deny yourself or others the gifts God has given you. Instead, you should give the job your best. Perhaps others somewhere could do a better job, but God values your availability. Through launching out, you will learn new things about yourself and gain a fuller understanding of your gifts and abilities.

Listening to Others
The people God places around us are like mirrors. They reflect

back to us, through their comments and insights, what our gifts and strengths are. While we should never be governed solely by another person's opinion of us, others can, nonetheless, prove valuable in assessing our strengths and weaknesses. Listen to what other people have to say about us, both the positive and negative. What do we receive the most compliments for? What do people see in us that we have not seen ourselves? Keep a record and begin to see what gifts others see in you.

Are you a good listener? Do people come to you with their problems? Perhaps you have a pastoral gift or a gift of mercy. As we learn more about our areas of strength and weakness, we can ask God where it is those strengths could be best used.

When people point out areas of weakness to us, we shouldn't dismiss it as slander. There is often much truth in their observations, even if their intent is dubious. Talk to the Lord about the things people say to you, especially if the same comment comes from more than one person. Take the initiative and discuss your weaknesses with others. Maybe you're not suited for what you are currently doing, and perhaps God wants to shift you into a job or ministry that will bring more fulfillment and fruit in your life, but he is waiting for you to humble yourself and admit your weaknesses.

The observations and insights of those around us are important if we are to have a balanced and accurate assessment of ourselves. To receive the full value of their input we must first listen to them, and then ask God for his input on the matter.

Being the Person God Intended
It is good to be inspired by others, but that is not to say we should try and imitate them. God created each of us uniquely

different from everyone else, and we insult him when we spend years trying to imitate others or contort ourselves into being something he never intended us to be. We each have many and varied gifts, and we will never discover exactly what they are if we're always copying others. The great moves of God in the past have been spearheaded by men and women who dared to be themselves.

During the last century, Hudson Taylor pioneered a new era in missions. His ideas were radical and unacceptable to the great majority of his peers. Undeterred by this, he persisted and founded the China Inland Mission which became the forerunner of many of today's missionary societies. Had Taylor been more concerned about the way others perceived him, he would never have left the shores of England. Instead, freed from self-doubt and the worry that no one else had ever done what he was about to do, he became all that God intended him to be—the father of much of our modern missionary endeavor.

The same is true of William Booth, founder of the Salvation Army. His challenge to the social ills of nineteenth-century England changed the course of a nation. Despite his success, Booth and the methods he employed were scorned by the Christians of his day. They felt he was too extreme and much too opinionated. But where would England be today if it had not been for the men and women of the Salvation Army?

Being all that God intended us to be is not always easy, but the rewards are always great.

Doing What You Enjoy

Sometimes when people come to me for advice on guidance I tell them: "Take seriously your natural desires. What do you enjoy doing? Do what you like!" They're often stunned by this, but they shouldn't be. God created each of us and if we have a desire to do something, and the abilities to carry it out, then he could well want us to do it for his glory. God does not give us talents and abilities only to taunt us.

In trying to discover what it is God wants us to do in life we sometimes overlook the obvious. This is particularly true of people who become Christians later in life. They can tend to associate all they've done in the past with their sinful lifestyle, and, in their desire to leave it all behind, sometimes fail to see that God has given them gifts to use for his kingdom. Because we have used our gifts outside the kingdom of God, this does not mean they're of no further use. Indeed, the opposite is true. However, our gifts first need to be sanctified and made available for use in the service of others.

Steve was a young man who had been heavily involved in Satanic rock music. He was an excellent guitarist, but after becoming a Christian gave away his guitar and vowed never to play it again. After several years of discipling he began to feel a yearning to buy another guitar and start playing again. He was cautious about this since he associated the guitar with his former lifestyle.

As he prayed, God showed him several things. First, every good gift comes from God, and he wanted Steve to use the gifts he had given him. Second, his musical talents had been given to him for a purpose, and by failing to acknowledge and use them, he was not being all God had created him to be. Steve saw that he had been blessed with musical talent, and simply because he had used it for the devil did not mean God no longer had a use for it.

Steve did go back to his musical career, and with strong Christian support has been an effective witness for Christ. His natural gift, coupled with God's anointing, are a powerful combination.

God has a special assignment for each of us. As we understand the gifts, strengths and abilities God has given us, we are in a better position to see areas where we are suited for service in his kingdom. Assess the desires of your heart to see if they are godly. Share them with those around you, and seek wise counsel. Above all, keep praying. Begin to use your gifts for the Lord.

As we serve others, as we make ourselves available to help where needed most, and as we offer the skills and gifts God has given us to serve in his kingdom as light in the world, we will become all he made us to be. That is his promise!

Hearing the Right Voice
The Bible teaches that there are three different sources or "voices" we can hear—the voice of God, of Satan and of sinful desires (or human desires that are good, but which may not be God's best for us). The task for us is to recognize and know which voice is which.

A voice that constantly tells us to avoid anything that places a demand on our lives and urges us to take the easy way out of things is most likely the voice of the flesh. This voice encourages us to pamper ourselves and listen to the promises of God without taking note of the conditions associated with them. God has promised to give us the desires of our hearts, but when our hearts are wholly his, our desires are also in harmony with his (Ps 37:4-5).

God wants us to seek him through prayer, submitting our thoughts and desires to him. Thus, when I am seeking God's direction, I like to express my need and dependence upon him to guide me. I consciously choose to set aside any selfish desires that would keep me from knowing his will. I also pray against Satan and ask God to protect me from his schemes. I exercise the authority we are given as believers to bind Satan and resist his influence and his evil ways (Jas 4:7; 1 Pet 5:8-9; Eph 6:10-20).

Since prayer is conversing with God, we should give God a chance to speak to us as well. There should be times of stillness and quiet, listening to God through meditation, Bible study and expectant silence. Do we pray without expecting God to speak to us? Do we believe he can speak to us? If so, should we not wait for him to speak?

We should never make a decision based on one impression in a time of prayer. We should test those impressions through seeking the counsel of godly people, reading God's Word, waiting for peace from the Lord in our hearts, and using our minds to analyze what God is leading us to do.

There have been times when my desires have not been in line with God's desires. In 1975 when I felt God wanted me to leave Amsterdam and move to the Dutch countryside, I did not want to go. I had been brought up in "the city" and was a "city boy" through and through. To me the city was where the action was, and I loved Amsterdam. The countryside was a nice place to visit for a week, but I had no desire to live there!

I struggled inside. Part of me said, "This is the will of God; he is leading me to the countryside." Yet another part said, "I'm doing something effective here. What good will sitting on a farm do me or anyone else?"

In the end I was honest with the Lord about my doubts and fears and lack of desire, and in that time of honesty I began to see things from God's perspective. This, in turn, changed the way I felt about the move he wanted me to make. A peace began to grow in my heart, as I began to see how the decision was consistent with goals and objectives we had set for our work.

Our attitude when seeking guidance is crucial. If we come to God in faith and humility, he promises to speak to us. But if we come with an attitude that we know what's best, we are more likely to hear the voice of Satan, the author of rebellious spirits.

The Bible teaches that Satan is an angel of light. He won't just tempt us with blatant sin but also with subtle deception. God seldom hurries us when he gives direction. Normally he allows us ample time to weigh the decision that must be made and come to a place of confidence about what he's asked us to do.

Conversely, Satan urges us to rush ahead without fully weighing and considering our choices. God guides, while Satan—and sometimes others as well—drives. So, if we feel an unnatural urgency about something to the extent that we don't even want to take the time to seek counsel or pray further about it, then we should be suspicious about whose voice we are really hearing. One thing Satan does not want us to do is to pray about things. "It is a snare for a man to say rashly, 'It is holy!' And after the vow to make inquiry" (Prov 20:25 NASB).

One of Satan's favorite tactics is confusion. If we're not sure about something, the best thing to do is wait. If it is the right thing to do, God will confirm it. Likewise, if after making a decision we believe to be in the will of God, we feel uneasy and confused, we should wait and ask God to confirm the decision to us.

God's voice has a liberating effect. Even when he asks us to do something difficult, there is a sense of confidence and expectancy about what lies ahead. We may not think it wise to share what he is asking us to do with everyone, but we should at least be able to share it with those we respect as mature Christians. If you cannot share your guidance with anyone else, beware— something is wrong.

When God Speaks

Most often, God speaks to those he has the confidence will do what he asks in the quietness of the heart. However, we should not put God in a box. He is free to guide us whenever, wherever and however he chooses. And when he speaks, he will not obscure things from us so that we have to puzzle over them for weeks trying to understand what it is he has said.

When God speaks, he is clear and specific. Do not get trapped into the practice of analyzing every event and circumstance that happens in life to see if God is speaking. From time to time God will use circumstances as a way of guiding us; however, we will know when those times are and will not have to go looking for them. God has promised to give us his peace, which "passes all understanding."

Questions for Individuals or Groups

1. What do you think are the spiritual gifts and natural abilities God has given you?

2. How have you put them to work?

3. What kinds of responses have you received from others about your gifts and abilities?

What do you receive compliments for? What gifts have others seen in you?

4. How do you react when someone points out a weakness in you? How can you make the best of such comments?

5. How can you make sure you don't think more of yourself than you ought or less than you ought (pp. 48-49)?

6. What do you enjoy doing?

How do you feel about the possibility that God may want you to do something for his glory that you enjoy?

7. The author mentions three voices we can hear—the voice of God, of Satan and of sinful desires (p. 53). How can we tell which voice is which?

8. From this chapter, what conclusions can you draw about what you can do to be all God wants you to be?

Five

Making Decisions

IMAGINE a young man taking a driving test. His instructor gives him one last piece of advice before he takes the test: "Tom, obey all road signs." Tom gets into the car with the examiner and waits. After a time, the examiner asks him if he knows how to start the car. Tom assures him he does and continues to wait. The examiner, becoming impatient, responds, "If this is some kind of game, I'm not amused. Either get the car started, or get out." Tom is shocked and tells the examiner that his driving instructor told him to obey all signs, so he is waiting for a sign to tell him to start the car.

"Ridiculous," you say. "Nobody could be that stupid." Yet, many of us are like that at times. We want to hear a voice booming from heaven telling us what to do next.

If Tom had started the car and driven off, he would have found road signs with instructions to obey. Even if he found no signs, that would be no excuse for him to stop driving since there are unposted road rules that must be obeyed for the safety of all. Similarly, in life there are times when we experience direct indisputable guidance and other times when we must simply follow the rules for living the Christian life. Through both means, we reach our destination of wholeheartedly submitting ourselves to Christ as Lord.

How can we then be sure that the decisions we make are in line with God's will for us? First, by carefully considering the pros and cons. This is a time to use some sanctified common sense. As you prepare to make an important decision, it is wise to list all the factors involved—such as:

Who would be affected?

How long would it take?

What changes would take place?

Why should there be a change?

What would be accomplished?

After you make the list, go through and prioritize the factors. What is the most important to you and why?

The following are principle-based questions to be asked prayerfully:

Will it honor God?

Will it help people?

Have I listened to wise counsel?

Have I included close friends?

What are my motives?

Can it be done with integrity?

Is it worth doing?

Can I do it in unity with those I fellowship with?

Do I have the gifts and abilities?

Is it the right time?

Is this decision consistent with the objectives God has shown me?

Would it undermine other commitments?

Fleeces

Some years after the Israelites moved into the Promised Land, they found themselves oppressed by the Midianites. So an angel of the Lord came to an Israelite named *Gideon* and told him, "Go in the strength you have and save Israel out of Midian's hand. Am I not sending you?" (Judg 6:14). The angel then caused a sacrifice to be burnt up instantly by only touching it with his staff. The angel immediately disappeared, but Gideon was still not convinced about what God wanted him to do.

So he placed a lamb's fleece on the ground overnight and asked God to saturate it with dew while the surrounding ground remained dry so he would know for sure God wanted him to fight the Midianites. And that is what happened. Still uncertain, he asked God to reverse the process the next night, leaving the fleece dry while the surrounding ground was wet with dew. And again it happened just as Gideon requested.

Why did Gideon do this? Because his life depended upon knowing what it was God wanted him to do and at what time. Gideon was about to lead Israel into a potentially devastating battle against the Midianites. Gideon used the fleece as a means of confirming what he already believed to be the will of God for the situation.

If we are to use fleeces in our guidance, then this is the proper context for their use. They are a means of confirming what already seems apparent to us as the will of God in a situation. They are not to be used as a way of getting fresh guidance from God. Though God can speak to us directly through "fleeces" we put before him, he wants to teach us to live by godly principles revealed in his Word. And he also wants to teach us to hear his voice, so that we can be guided by the Holy Spirit in those tough situations where we have to choose between two or three equally good possibilities. Seeking the Lord through "fleeces" can be an indication of a lack of faith or a lack of sound teaching. God wants us to grow in maturity and wisdom so that the decisions we make in life can be directed by biblical principles or hearing God's voice directly to our minds and hearts.

I heard of a young man who had to drive through a set of streetlights on his way to college. Each morning he would pray: "God, if you want me at school today make the light green. If it's red I'll assume you want me to play racquetball instead." That is not a biblical fleece!

Financial Confirmation

God can also confirm his will by providing us with adequate finances. If you are planning a new venture but do not have the necessary funds to cover it, ask God to confirm its rightness by giving you the needed money. However, finances are for confirmation, not guidance—that comes only from the Lord.

My first foreign outreach with Youth with A Mission was in Jamaica. My father and I discussed the prospect of my going, and while he was behind my desire to go, he made it clear that it was not going to be my faith and his finances that got me there! (Later, as I grew in my faith, I saw how wise his counsel was.)

After talking with my father, a phrase I'd heard came to mind, "If you do the possible, God will do the impossible." I set about raising as much money as I could. My friends and I collected used household items from friends and neighbors, and we had a garage sale. I took my old basketball trophies and tried to sell them, but I quickly found out nobody wants secondhand trophies!

As I did this, God began to release the finances I needed. The most humbling experience was when R. T. Cummings, a friend in my church, signed his monthly injury compensation check over to me. It was all his family had to live on for the next month. R. T. insisted, saying if I had the faith to go, then he had the faith to stay. "I can trust God just like you can," he declared.

I boarded the bus in Los Angeles with enough money to get me as far as Miami. I would travel there, and if the Lord provided the rest of my fare along the way, I would fly on to Jamaica.

From a bus depot in Texas I called my father who told me excitedly of a non-Christian relative who had just visited him. He had told the relative about my trip but made no mention of my financial needs since he had assumed the relative would not be interested in helping. But to his surprise the relative had offered to write a check for me. Neither of them knew how much I needed, so I was both surprised and excited when I found out that my relative's check covered my remaining travel costs and other expenses to the last penny.

I traveled on to Jamaica with a sense of awe in my heart. I knew I was in the center of God's will. Not only had God worked on my behalf, but R. T. Cummings, who had given so sacrificially to me, also saw God provide food, funds and clothing. The Cummings family had not lacked for one thing during the whole month I was gone.

There have been many more financial tests along the way, but as a teen-ager on my first overseas outreach, I learned firsthand that God will provide if we just step out in faith. I did not step out presumptuously. I knew God wanted me to attend that outreach, and I did my part as well, so his provision was indeed a confirmation to me of his will. The principle of doing the possible and trusting God for the impossible had become real to me.

Scriptures
God can use his Word to speak to us. It can speak to our situation through our daily readings, or God can impress specific passages on our minds as we wait upon him in prayer.

It is important, however, not to make the mistake of interpreting the meaning of the passage by how it is used to speak to us in a specific situation. Sometimes God is gracious enough to speak to us from passages out of context, but that does not constitute a principle interpreting Scripture.

Peace
God will also give peace to our hearts when we are doing his will. His presence brings peace. When we have prayed and thought through a decision, we can expect God to confirm the right choice with a peace that gives us confidence even in the midst of difficulty.

Dreams and Visions
God can also use dreams and visions. They can confirm what

we already believe to be the will of God for us. If a dream seems to be fresh guidance, we should seek other confirmation of the guidance from God. The realm of dreams and visions is very subjective, and if we do not take these precautions, Satan can easily confuse us.

Jeff was a young man who felt God wanted him to work with a specific ministry within Youth With A Mission. He wrote to the ministry explaining how he felt called and asked for an application form. Several weeks went by and there was no reply.

Then one night Jeff had a dream. In the dream he received a letter from the ministry which he opened. Inside was an application form and a cover letter which told him that while they had enclosed an application form, there was no chance of his being able to join the ministry in the foreseeable future. Jeff also heard a voice telling him he would receive just such a letter from the ministry the next day, but that he was not to pay attention to its discouraging message. Instead, he was to fill out the application form and take it to the ministry in person.

The next morning Jeff was waiting for the mail to arrive, and sure enough there was his letter from the ministry. He anxiously tore it open and inside was a letter that read almost exactly as he had seen in his dream. It said there was an accommodation shortage and as a result they were unable to take on any new staff. Jeff was elated.

His friends found it hard to understand that he was so excited about being turned down. They did not realize the letter was God's confirmation to him that he would be part of the ministry. He filled out the application and did as the Lord had instructed him to do with it. Jeff was accepted on to the staff within three weeks and still serves with Youth With A Mission today—more than ten years later! The dream confirmed to Jeff that his guidance was right and gave him the encouragement he needed to pursue it.

Cautions Regarding Guidance

The following are some important principles to keep in mind:

1. Don't plan your life around a preconceived idea of what God's plan is for you. Seek security and direction in a person, not in a detailed program. We need a guide, not a road map, and Jesus is that guide.

2. Obey the truth you know as a basis for knowing God's will for the future.

3. There are times when it is not clear what to do next in life. Sometimes God will test us to see if we trust him and will walk in faith. Always obey the last thing God called you to do until he shows you the next.

4. Don't make demands or set deadlines with God.

5. When going through a rough time, don't doubt what God has directed you to do previously. In other words, when you're in a time of spiritual darkness, don't turn away from what God has shown you in the light.

6. Don't be proud. Don't say, "If this is not God's will, I have never heard his voice." We can all make mistakes. Be prepared to admit you are wrong. That is our greatest protection!

7. Don't use the wrong means for the right end. Cheating in exams to get a degree to serve God is not God's will.

8. Don't confuse hormones with holiness. How often have we heard the words, "God told me I was to marry him," and it was not God's will?

9. Don't confuse the "movement" with the "moment." Seek

God's timing as well as the right thing to do.

10. Don't become superspiritual. Learn to be practical as well as to be open to hearing God's voice. If he speaks to you, he will confirm his voice through other godly people.

11. Don't act independently. Be a person who is accountable to others.

12. Don't get caught up in spiritual verbosity. Be practical and wise in the way you communicate your desire to do God's will. Using common-sense expressions and terms to express our sense of guidance helps keep us balanced. Besides, declaring that God has told us to do something may not only be pride, it may also cut off a process of discussion and counsel with other Christians. It is hard to help persons who declare unequivocally that God has told them to do something.

Unfulfilled Promises

What should we do when we feel we have had a definite promise from God that has not yet come to pass? There are many instances in Scripture where a considerable amount of time lapsed between a promise and its fulfillment. In fact, the rule seems to be promise plus preparation equals fulfillment. After God has given us a promise, he sets about preparing us to receive it.

If we study the lives of any of the great Bible characters, we see this truth illustrated over and over again. Consider the lapse of time between God telling Noah about the flood and the actual occurrence of that flood. Yet, it was knowledge of the flood and the promise that his family would be spared that propelled Noah to build the ark. The promise was given, Noah completed the required work, and the promise was fulfilled.

Jesus told Peter he would be a rock. However, Peter had

much preparation to go through before that promise was fulfilled. Likewise, the rest of the disciples had three-and-a-half years of learning and testing before they were ready for all God had promised them. When we have a promise from God, we should hold on to it, cooperate in any needed preparation and allow the *Lord* to bring the fulfillment of the promise.

Another aspect of timing and the will of God is waiting for God's opportunity. In college I played basketball. My team was especially eager one season to play against the University of Florida because one of their players was being considered as an All-American. We expected a tall and muscular player, but to our surprise he wasn't. Indeed, from first appearances there seemed to be little that was remarkable about him.

As the game commenced, I noticed that he wasn't even fast on his feet. But he possessed an uncanny ability to be in the right place at the right time. If a team was moving one way and the ball bouncing another, he was right there where the ball was. His hands were up to catch the ball when they should be, and if it came bouncing to the floor, he was there to pick it up. It made him a great player.

God wants us to be like that basketball player. He wants us to have the spiritual alertness that puts us in the right place at the right time when the Spirit is wanting to do something. As we seek his direction, we need to distinguish between the right thing to do and the right time to do it. God may put a plan or desire in our hearts, but we should not presume that means we do it immediately. God may be preparing our hearts, and we are to take plenty of time to think, discuss and ponder what he is stirring in our hearts.

Guidance from Christian Leaders

God may, at times, use a leader to give us guidance or confirm something he has been saying to us. Once, an internationally recognized Bible teacher was ministering in a group I was working with. I can still recall her, as she prayed with the group of people, going over to one young couple and giving them some specific counsel she felt God had laid on her heart for them. They were somewhat confused by what she said, so later they talked further with the woman. They said, "What you said to us doesn't make any sense."

I watched for her reaction. Graciously, with no hint of self-defense, she replied: "I felt strongly that I needed to share that with you, but I could be wrong. I've been wrong before. Submit it to the Lord. If it is from him, he will confirm it in other ways. If it is not, then I apologize."

As I listened, I thought, "Here's a woman who isn't afraid of being wrong. She's not pushing her ministry as the infallible Word of God." My admiration for and confidence in her ministry grew greatly. We can all be wrong at times, but it takes people who fear God more than their reputations to admit to it.

No leaders, regardless of how well-known and trusted they are, can make our decisions for us. We are responsible before God for our own guidance, and it is both dangerous and foolish to take that responsibility lightly, or abdicate it altogether and let another do it for us.

If we hear a leader claim to hear the voice of God for others and then encourage them to act quickly on it, loud warning bells should sound in our ears. We must never allow another to violate our sense of caution and intuition and bully us into doing something we're unsure of. God watches over us, and we must never allow anyone to take his place. The results of doing so can be disastrous.

The tragedy of people who are slavishly in bondage to cults bears witness to this. They have unreservedly handed their personal freedom and responsibility over to someone who claims to have cornered the market on spiritual truth. As time goes by, they lose their ability to think clearly and make decisions for themselves. They are psychological cripples addicted to the pseudospiritual platitudes their human god feeds them.

Biblical Guidance

This is not what God intended. He created our minds and he expects us to use them. Indeed it is he who says, "Come now, let us reason together" (Is 1:18). He wants us to serve him not out of some slavish bondage whereby we surrender to him even our ability to think; he wants us to serve him because we have reasoned together and have come to see and understand that he is right and that he is worthy of our allegiance.

Hearing God's voice in specific guidance does not necessarily signify spirituality or God's stamp of approval. On the contrary, a study of the Bible reveals that spectacular guidance is often reserved for the hardheaded and rebellious.

In Numbers 22—24 we read of Balak's messengers who ask the prophet Balaam to come and curse Israel. So Balaam goes with the men. But while on the journey, his donkey stops and refuses to go on. Balaam is furious but finally realizes that the donkey saw an angel blocking the way that Balaam did not see.

Consider Balaam and his donkey. When the angel finally got Balaam's attention, he told him he would sooner have killed him than talk to him! With that introduction the angel went on to give specific instructions to Balaam about what to say when he reached Balak. Obviously it was not Balaam's spirituality that singled him out for God's special direction. It was his rebellion!

Likewise Saul, on the road to Damascus, received a vision and was temporarily blinded. We think of Saul simply as a great man of God. But he was not great at that stage. He was a ruthless hater of Christians who was present when Stephen was stoned to death. God did not single him out because he was righteous, but because of the unrighteousness he wanted to change.

There are also many recorded instances where God gives spiritually mature men and women guidance to carry out specific tasks. The book of Acts has many such inspiring examples: Paul's call to Macedonia, and Peter's vision of the unclean foods and subsequent visit to Cornelius's house.

Sometimes guidance is given as a stamp of approval and other times as a mark of discipline. We must always remember that we cannot force God's hand as to how he will deliver guidance, and we must be wary of making heroes of those God guides in more spectacular ways than others.

The Bottom Line of Guidance

"My shield is with God, who saves the upright in heart" (Ps 7:10 NASB).

There are pitfalls in the area of guidance. For every method of guidance, we can name someone who has tried it and failed. But therein lies the problem: Guidance is not some kind of horoscope or divining rod we pull out every time we want to know something about the future. Guidance is purely and simply God communicating to us about very specific matters. Nothing, not even our desire to serve God, is to undermine a pure and simple devotion to Jesus.

Most of God's will for our lives is already revealed in the Bible. The point of this chapter is not to provide us with methods of guidance, but to illuminate ways God can speak to us and to help us recognize when he does. The only effective method of guidance I know is living our lives wholeheartedly for God. If we do this, then assuredly *we will know his guidance in our lives*. He wants to guide us more than we want to be guided. The most important things to God are our openness to obey him and a teachable spirit.

Each of us needs God's direction in life, and should he choose to lead us by way of a different route than we are presently on, we must be willing to follow. It is easier to change the direction of something already in motion than something that is stationary. As every parent can attest, it's easier to get the child who is cleaning the car to stop and run an errand than it is to get the child who is lazy to do it. Likewise, if we are striving to hear God's voice and, at the same time, doing our best to please him, then we are more likely to hear his voice and respond to it.

"Trust in the LORD with all your heart and lean not on your own understanding; in all your ways acknowledge him, and he will make your paths straight" (Prov 3:5-6).

Where Do We Go from Here?

We have seen that there is a place for both general and specific guidance in the Christian life, and that one should not be emphasized at the expense of the other. I like to think of guidance and the Christian life this way.

Imagine I receive an invitation to visit my friend who lives at 270 Imperial Road, Madras, India. If I accept the invitation, the first thing I do is not to go and buy a map of Madras to locate Imperial Road. Instead I make reservations for a flight to India. Once I get to India, I make my way to Madras and once I'm in Madras, I locate Imperial Road. After arriving at Imperial Road, I find number 270 where my friend lives.

Our Christian life is a journey. We can make the mistake of focusing so closely on the specifics of the journey that we fail to see the broad picture. The specifics are there, just as 270 Imperial Road is in Madras. However, unless I get to Madras, any street map with the specific location of Imperial Road on it is of little use to me.

All of us would like to know where we will be and what we'll be doing ten years from now, but we must live in the reality of where we are today. Our security is to be in a person, not a plan.

As we begin to move in the direction we feel God is leading us, we listen and ask God for more specific directions. We may not always be certain of our final destination, but we are always certain of how God wants us to conduct ourselves on the journey, and we can be absolutely and totally confident of his love for us and his commitment to direct our lives. Our ultimate victory is assured—as long as we keep our hearts open to the Lord Jesus. God has a plan for our lives, and once we are moving he can lead us into it.

" 'For I know the plans I have for you,' declares the LORD, 'plans to prosper you and not to harm you, plans to give you hope and a future' " (Jer 29:11).

Questions for Individuals or Groups

1. What is difficult for you about seeking God's guidance?

2. Note the questions listed on pages 60-61. How could these be helpful to you as you face an important decision?

3. The author gives the example of Gideon, who used a fleece to confirm God's will (p. 61). Why did Gideon use a fleece and what are the potential dangers we might encounter in using this method for guidance?

4. How can finances indicate God's will (pp. 62-64)?

5. On pages 64-65, the author mentions dreams and visions as potential channels for hearing God's voice. How do you respond to this?

6. As you look at the cautions listed on page 66, which do you find to be an especially helpful reminder? Explain.

7. Have you ever felt like God has not come through with a promise he made (pp. 67-68)? Describe it.

How do you respond to the author's comment that even in Scripture God did not always fulfill a promise immediately?

8. What can be the dangers of following the guidance of a Christian leader too closely (pp. 68-70)?

9. The author closes the chapter by saying, "Our security is to be in a person, not a plan" (p. 73). What does this mean to you?

10. Consider one decision in your life you are making now that you would like God's direction for. What principles from this chapter could help you make that decision? Explain.

Six

Whom Do
We Serve?

IMAGINE that I wrote Sally (my wife) asking her to marry me, and her response was something like this:

Dear Floyd,

I would love to marry you. It's a dream come true. Thank you. There are a few minor details, though.

I have a couple of other boyfriends—well, ten to be exact. Most of them don't mean much to me, but can I keep Fred and Dennis? I must be in love, because I've never before been willing to give up so many of my boyfriends! Mom says you're a lucky man!

There's one other thing. I will accept your proposal on the condition that I can stay in Texas and live with my parents. I love them. They have done so much for me that I couldn't dream of leaving them. You wouldn't want me to hurt their feelings, would you? However, you can visit whenever you want. I'm sure you'll understand.

I look forward to setting the wedding date!

Yours in undying love and devotion,

Sally

If I had received that kind of reply from Sally to my marriage proposal, I would not have married her. I don't think any of us would! When I asked Sally to marry me, I expected that she would lay aside all others for me, and I would do likewise. That is what marriage is about—committing ourselves wholeheartedly to the other person. We would feel cheated if our partner suggested any other kind of relationship than this.

How then does God feel when we say, "Lord, I love you so much that I'm going to give up everything in my life except John"—or Kathy or my stereo or my car or my job or whatever else is important? Or we say, "I want to serve you, but please don't send me to the mission field. I couldn't do that to my family!"

We're told in James 1:8 that, a "double-minded" person is "unstable in all he does." Double-mindedness leads to frustration and undermines the power God wants to give us. God longs to pour his Spirit into our lives and give us the motivation and ability to make right choices in life. He doesn't demand a certain level of maturity, intellectual ability or recognition from our peers before he will do this. What he requires is our total, unswerving commitment to him. It is not abilities that impress God, but availability.

Total commitment seems easy in church on Sunday morning. But putting Jesus first in our lives has to be worked out on a daily basis. It has to be lived out in the face of constant pressure to conform to the spirit of this world. This pressure can come from a myriad of different sources: from friends, acquaintances, people we work with or go to school with, and through the media. However, Jesus wants to give us the strength to withstand this pressure so that we can live our lives to love and please him.

Paul speaks of this tension: "Don't you know that when you offer yourselves to someone to obey him as slaves, you are slaves to the one whom you obey—whether you are slaves to sin, which leads to death, or to obedience, which leads to righteousness?" (Rom 6:16). He asserts that every one of us is a slave to somebody! Some of us are love slaves, and some of us are sin slaves. Whom do we serve? We cannot serve two masters.

Paul goes on to say, "But thanks be to God that though you used to be slaves to sin, you wholeheartedly obeyed the form of teaching to which you were entrusted" (Rom 6:17). So, though we were once slaves to our passions, desires, fears and hurts, we have now been set free. No longer do we have to be enslaved to those things that once held us prisoner.

Count the Cost
You can be free from the power of sin! But there is a price to pay.

Jesus told a parable of a man who went to build a tower but did not have enough money to complete it. He said the man should have sat down and calculated the cost before starting. It would have saved embarrassment and wasted effort. "So therefore," Jesus says, "whoever of you does not renounce all that he has cannot be my disciple" (Lk 14:33 RSV).

Christians must pause and count the cost of putting God first in their lives. If we are not ready to make that total commitment, then we need to admit to ourselves that we will never enter into and enjoy victorious Christian living.

There are accounts of the great nineteenth-century American evangelist Charles Finney refusing people who begged him to pray for their salvation. He told them they needed more time to repent before God and consider the seriousness of their conversion. This may seem hard but, as a result, Finney had a very high rate of converts who zealously lived for Christ all their lives. This happened because he did all that was possible to ensure their full repentance first. I wonder sometimes if much of the "backsliding" we hear of today happens because we have eased people into conversion without repentance or relinquishment.

Victory over What?

Many Christians have spent years trying to defeat something they little understand! In order to grasp a better understanding of sin we need to examine what sin is not. Sin is *not* simply disobeying an arbitrary set of rules.

My friend David, full of newfound faith and enthusiasm for the Lord, joined a church and was immediately handed a 130-page rulebook! Covered in it was everything from where he could go and when, to what clothes to wear, how long his hair could be and even whom he could associate with. Tragically, the rulebook dealt with everything except what really mattered— heart attitudes and Christian character. The implication of the rulebook was that if you followed all the rules, you were making it as a Christian. If not, you were out!

I wonder sometimes if Jesus would have kept all those rules. He spoke scathingly of the Pharisees because they had reduced relationship with God to a set of detailed and often ridiculous regulations. Yet there are some leaders who unfortunately think the way to make people holy is to load them down with a long list of do's and don'ts. This approach, however, only produces guilt and condemnation. The more rules there are, the greater our sense of failure when we are unable to live up to them all.

Jesus made a clear distinction between temptation and sin. Temptation to sin is not sin, but we often think it is. This is a confusion that plays right into the devil's hands. Satan loves us to believe we've sinned when in fact we have only been tempted.

Jesus was tempted in the wilderness, yet we are told he was without sin. He did not give in to the temptation. Jesus did not leave the wilderness with feelings of defeat and unworthiness. He was tempted, just as we are, when Satan presented him with thoughts of power, wealth, recognition—shortcuts to becoming all that God wanted him to be. But he did not bow to those temptations and so did not sin.

If we have nagging feelings of guilt, then we need to ask ourselves: "Have I sinned? What specifically did I do wrong, and how can I correct it?" We need to ask God to reveal these things to us. He is committed to helping us lead victorious lives and will show us our sins if we ask him to.

If, after you have done this, nothing comes to mind, then quite possibly Satan is attacking you with vague accusations of sin. If you are feeling false condemnation which leaves you powerless and joyless, go to a mature Christian and pray it through together.

When the Holy Spirit convicts us of sin it will be clear what we have done wrong. Condemnation is often vague and related to a general sense of failure rather than a specific sin. False feelings based on the accusation of the enemy can destroy us. However, when the Holy Spirit convicts those who are open to him, the conviction will be accompanied by a realization of God's grace and the hope that belongs to those who belong to Jesus Christ. The purpose of guilt is to show us that we have done wrong and to bring us to Jesus!

Paul tells us to resist the devil (and his temptations), and he will flee from us. It is when we entertain temptation and allow it to grow in our minds that sin is produced. If we are tempted and are actively resisting it, then we are not sinning. It is when we welcome it, entertain it and give into it that we have entered into sin.

Sin is not a product of our environment and beyond our control. Many people believe certain sins are beyond their control and justify it with excuses such as "I hate all men. My father molested me when I was twelve." Or one might say: "All I heard was criticism when I was growing up. Don't tell me I should encourage my wife—it's just not the way that I was brought up." Such past experiences are tragic, and dealing with them is tremendously difficult. But they are not an excuse for sin.

I have heard some people say that the "devil made them do it" as if they had no choice in the matter. Neither the enemy nor sin can tempt us in a way that we cannot overcome. The Bible promises that with every temptation the Lord will make a way of escape (1 Cor 10:13). Our challenge is not to focus on the sin or the tempter, but on the way of escape!

In the Old Testament God made it clear to the Jews that they could not blame others for their sin. Instead, they were to take responsibility for their own thoughts and actions:

The word of the LORD came to me again: "What do you mean by repeating this proverb concerning the land of Israel, 'The fathers have eaten sour grapes, and the children's teeth are set on edge'? As I live, says the Lord GOD, this proverb shall no more be used by you in Israel. Behold, all souls are mine; the soul of the father as well as the soul of the son is mine: the soul that sins shall die." (Ezek 18:1-4 RSV).

God will hold those who sin responsible for their sin and will allow no excuses for sin.

God has not only given us commandments to keep, but he has given us the power to obey them. He makes that clear in his words to Cain after the Fall, "The LORD said to Cain, 'Why are you angry? Why is your face downcast? If you do what is right, will you not be accepted? But if you do not do what is right, sin is crouching at your door; it desires to have you, but you must master it' " (Gen 4:6).

Sin and Emotional Pain

Being emotionally hurt by a friend or family member is not a sin. However, we must be aware that emotional wounds can easily become an occasion to sin. It is like a crack in a dam. If it is left unchecked, it will cause the whole dam to collapse. When somebody hurts us deeply, we can either respond in hatred and bitterness and develop a critical, divisive spirit, or we can ask God to fill us with his love and not allow bitterness and an unclean spirit to develop in our hearts.

Jesus told us to bless those who curse us. If we don't consciously make this effort and invite the Holy Spirit into the situation, then the wrong done to us will produce a harvest of sin in our lives. We are responsible for our reactions to the pain we experience in our lives. It is our choice, and God will hold us accountable.

Sin always produces hurt, always robs us of the joy of close fellowship, whether that is with our heavenly Father or with our family and friends. Sin does not occur in a vacuum, but widens its effects on the lives of many others.

Sin is more than outward action. Jesus talked much about sin, and more often in the context of inward attitudes than outward actions. He said, "Not what enters into the mouth defiles the man, but what proceeds out of the mouth, this defiles the man. . . . But the things that proceed out of the mouth come from the heart, and those defile the man" (Mt 15:11,18 NASB).

We often focus on outward sins—sins of commission—but there are also sins of the heart, secret sins, secret thoughts. Jesus contended that persons who plot sin but do not carry it out are just as guilty as if they had committed the act. If, for example, a businessman plans to commit adultery with a coworker, but on the way to the hotel she has an accident and can't make the rendezvous, in his heart he is guilty of the sin of adultery, even though he did not physically commit that sin.

God holds us accountable for the intent of our hearts in a way that stands in stark contrast to the world's thinking. Imagine someone being brought to court for privately contemplating stealing the petty-cash box from his or her employer. It could not be done because we cannot read other's minds and know what they are thinking. However, God can read our minds! "Man looks at the outward appearance, but the LORD looks at the heart" (1 Sam 16:7). Moreover, Jesus promises that the things we think in private will one day be shouted from the rooftops!

By examining what sin is not, we gain a clearer picture of what it is. It is deliberate violation, either by thought or action, of what we know to be right and true in our heart and conscience. Sin is breaking God's moral laws. It is giving in to temptation when, at the root of our being, we know it is wrong and will ultimately bring pain to ourselves and others. It is rebellion against God, for by willingly committing sin we are saying to God, "I know it's wrong and you don't approve of it, but I want it!" Our sin brings heartache and pain to the God of love who created us for himself.

Throughout Christian history, there has been much debate as to whether we, as humans, have to sin. Is there a genetic reason for sin, or is it strictly a choice each individual makes? For each of us personally, this argument is beside the point. Instead we should be asking, "Have I sinned?" If so, let's deal with the reality of our failure and not get into a long theological controversy about why people sin. The fact of the matter is that we all do sin. The Bible says very simply, "all have sinned and fall short of the glory of God" (Rom 3:23). I believe every human has ratified Adam's rebellion. Every person is sinful by nature. What is important is that we accept responsibility for our sinfulness and not blame it on others.

Despite the seeming hopelessness of humanity's universal selfishness, there is hope. God has not abandoned us to sin, but has provided a wonderful means of reconciliation and forgiveness—his Son, Jesus. Through the atoning death and subsequent resurrection of Jesus Christ, we can be set wonderfully free, no longer enslaved to the power of death. This is not to say that we will always be free from the enticement of sin, but it provides us with the means of winning the struggle with sin and entering into the victorious Christian life. The principles set out in the next chapters are weapons that each one of us can employ in that ongoing struggle to live a victorious Christian life.

Questions for Individuals or Groups

1. How is commitment to Christ like marriage (pp. 75-76)?

2. How do pressures from friends, coworkers or the media push us away from total commitment to Christ?

3. The apostle Paul in Romans 6:16 seems to imply that the choice is not between being enslaved or free, but rather who we will be a slave to—sin or obedience (p. 77). How do you respond to this idea?

4. Do you agree or disagree with Charles Finney's practice of refusing potential converts until they had adequately repented (p. 78)? Explain.

5. Why is it so easy to confuse Christian maturity with following a set of rules (pp. 78-79)?

6. Many of us have been sinned against in ways that have had long-lasting effects on us. McClung says, "Such past experiences are tragic, and dealing with them is tremendously difficult. But they are not an excuse for sin" (p. 80). Do you agree or disagree? Explain.

7. How can we prevent these emotional hurts from developing into bitterness or anger (pp. 81-83)? Is forgiveness a one-time event? Why or why not?

Seven

Open
to God

JESUS is Lord. So where do I start living under his lordship? John wrote, "If we walk in the light, as he is in the light, we have fellowship with one another, and the blood of Jesus, his Son, purifies us from all sin" (1 Jn 1:7). We sing about walking in the light. The phrase adorns posters, napkin holders and T-shirts. Yet despite its usage in popular Christian culture, I wonder if many of us really know what is meant by "walking in the light."

The phrase has a very spiritual sound to it, but it is also very down-to-earth. It means living in a state of honesty, with desires of our hearts known to both God and others.

Imagine that the angel Gabriel is sent to you with a special "moral Polaroid camera." This camera can take pictures of your thought life when there is unconfessed sin. These photographs can then be developed and sold through mail order or at the front of your church for twenty-five cents a piece.

How would you feel about the above scenario? Are you happy for people to know your secret thoughts?

Before we lapse into depression over this prospect, we need to acknowledge that all of us struggle in our thoughts with anger, disappointment and other negative emotions. It is human to have feelings, and God does not want us to deny them. However, he does want us to be honest with him about sin. Walking in the light depends not on whether or not God knows our sin—he does—but on whether or not we tell him.

Being Honest with God

Suppose Fred is falsifying the accounts of the company he works for. His employer realizes this is going on but does not challenge him on it. This does not mean Fred is being honest with his employer. Whether his employer knows of his actions is not the issue. Only when Fred confesses his actions is he being honest. Likewise, John tells us, "If we confess our sins, he is faithful and just and will forgive us our sins and purify us from all unrighteousness" (1 Jn 1:9).

I live in Amsterdam, Holland, where God has called me to a ministry with youth and with street people of all kinds. Where I work pornography abounds and prostitutes sit in picture windows trying to lure customers. As I walk up and down those streets day after day, I have found one of the best ways of keeping my thoughts pure and clean is to remind myself that I am continually in God's presence. It is God who has called me to work in this area. I'm not just an inquisitive tourist peering into windows or trying to catch a glimpse of what lies behind the well-guarded brothel doors.

If an unclean thought does come to mind, there are two things I have to do. First, I have to be honest with myself. If I am thinking an unclean thought, I need to say to myself, "Floyd, that is impure and you don't want it." Second, I must bring the thought to Jesus. This act of bringing something to Jesus is what the Bible calls "walking in the light."

There is power in the light. There are no pockets of darkness in a well-lit room. Darkness only exists if an object blocks out the light and causes a shadow. Refusing to admit our sins is one way in which we cast shadows in our spiritual lives. If we are not careful to remove those shadows by acknowledging our sins, we will have darkness in our lives.

We need to come into the presence of a holy God and say: "God, here are my thoughts. They are ugly and impure, and I need your help. I don't want them." When we do this with each and every sinful thought, we allow Jesus to break into our lives and bring his help and light into the struggle.

When I confess my sins to Jesus he doesn't respond with: "You did what? I'm shocked! That's the worst sin I've ever heard of!" Ecclesiastes tells us there is nothing new under the sun, and nothing could be more true. Read the Old and New Testaments and you will find any number of sins and failures. But read too of the God who forgives, who picks us up and puts our feet on solid ground. He loves us, and for our ultimate good wants us to be honest before him by confessing our sins. If we humble ourselves, walk in the light and are willing to be known for who we really are, then he is willing and ready to help us.

Confess Your Sins to One Another

God will direct us to mature Christians (who do not have the same problem we have), and he wants us to open up to them. At times like these, the devil may try to trick us by whispering such things as, "I can't tell anybody that—it's too bad!" Or, "No one will ever talk to me again if they know that about me!" These lies keep us from confession, and we must not listen to them.

There is a false kind of rationalizing that says, "My sins are under the blood of Jesus, so nobody else needs to know about them." This is a half-truth which fails to acknowledge our need to confess our sins to one another. Telling other Christians about our sins does not provide for our forgiveness; only the death of Jesus on the cross is sufficient to forgive us our sins.

But confessing our sins to others allows us to walk in the light, making it all the more difficult for the enemy to get the upper hand over us. It also assures us of God's love when others know us completely and are still able to accept us. This is a manifestation of God's love and grace.

Think of all we would have missed if the Bible only recorded the triumphs of its characters. How would we understand some of David's psalms if we did not know of his sin with Bathsheba? And knowing of it, how much more the beauty and grace revealed in Psalm 51 can minister to us in times of need.

It's not a sin to be weak! However, it is folly and sometimes sin to struggle alone when, through the commitment of other Christians, God has provided us with his love for our support. Christian maturity means coming to a place of acknowledging our weaknesses as an opportunity for growth. Paul clearly grasped this point when he wrote that God's " 'power is made perfect in weakness.' Therefore I will boast all the more gladly about my weaknesses, so that Christ's power may rest on me" (2 Cor 12:9).

In the Garden of Gethsemane Jesus himself struggled with his emotions and eventually won the victory over them. And many of us like to read about Peter because we find ourselves mirrored in his personal struggles. We find ourselves rejoicing at his successes and agonizing over his failures.

There is a tendency for those who have been Christians for some time or who hold positions of spiritual leadership to convey the impression that they are beyond temptation. This is a dangerous situation, both for those who think it and for the younger Christians who may believe them. All of us, regardless of our years or position, are going to face temptation and struggle in our lives. There is potential for sin in the heart of every person, and only by taking that seriously and being accountable to others who are walking in the light with the Lord Jesus can we have victory over sin.

In the Bible the Christian life is often compared to a human lifespan. A baby first learns to sit, then stand, and finally starts to walk, skip and run. If a child goes on for year after year not learning how to walk, we know something is seriously wrong and corrective action is needed.

Today there are many Christians faking it. They are acting happy and spiritual on the outside, but on the inside they struggle with all manner of issues. They have not learned to walk and run spiritually. It is time to take off the mask and begin experiencing real joy built on the foundation of godly humility. True spirituality and the seeds of victory come from being honest when we are defeated or discouraged.

Flee—Don't Flirt
Paul tells us to "make no provision for the flesh in regard to

its lusts" (Rom 13:14 NASB). To put it another way, this means we are not to deliberately put ourselves in a place of temptation, either to prove how strong we are or because we are denying we have a weakness in a particular area of our lives. Christians must flee temptation, not flirt with it. It is not common sense to continually present our areas of weakness with temptation.

I love eating ice cream—chocolate-coated ice cream bars, sundaes, ice cream cakes, ice cream cones and even ice cream right out of the carton! Imagine that I was trying to stop eating ice cream altogether. To impress my wife with my self-control, I would ask her to make homemade double-chocolate ice cream with walnuts and almonds! I ask her to leave several scoops of it in bowls around the house: one beside my bed so I can see it when I go to sleep, another in the bathroom to tantalize me while I shave in the morning. Everywhere I turn I want to see ice cream! If I open the refrigerator door, I want to see a bowl of ice cream with my name on it, and all because I want to impress my wife by resisting temptation at every turn!

Such a scheme would be ridiculous! If I don't want to eat ice cream, then why torture myself by having it constantly before me? If I am proving anything at all, it is how foolish I am. Alcoholics Anonymous does not encourage those trying to break free of the bondage of alcohol to sit night after night in bars to prove they have overcome their problem—a devastating result would be inevitable. Areas of weakness in our lives are difficult enough to overcome without added exposure to temptation.

We have a policy in our mission in Amsterdam. We ask our workers not to witness to prostitutes alone. None of us is above temptation or sin, and we do not want to give any room to it.

If we do, it will surely raise its ugly head!

I believe it's common sense that people should not counsel those of the opposite sex alone. Pastors and those with counseling ministries in particular can get tripped up by this. When pastors, who are having difficult times in their marriages, counsel attractive and vulnerable persons of the opposite sex—who keep telling the pastors they are "the most sensitive persons they have ever talked with"—they have placed themselves in a position of weakness. Many are able to stand against this subtle temptation, but others give in with devastating consequences. Do not create *any opportunity* for the flesh to prevail.

At the same time we must be careful not to shy away from the opportunities God brings our way. If a woman comes to a pastor's office in deep distress and pours out her heart, he shouldn't feel he has to stop her mid-sentence and arrange a meeting for the next week when his wife will be around.

The wisest thing for pastors or counselors to do is to open the door to their offices, ask their secretaries or someone else to join them, or sit in an open place where everyone can see them. They could then listen to the person's immediate problems and afterward invite him or her over to their home to speak with their spouses and themselves. The point is not to refuse to deal with the woman and her problem, but to look for ways to avoid temptation while helping her.

If someone has a problem with gossip and spends hours with others who also love to gossip, he or she needs to find some new friends who aren't so inclined. We need to plan things to do when we are with others so there won't be long lulls in the conversation that we fill with other people's business.

If our weakness is getting too physically involved on dates, then why continue being alone together in the car night after night? Why always plan dates that don't involve others? All too often we wait until sin is right within our reach before seeing whether we have the self-control to avoid it.

Recently, a young man named *Kevin* told me he thanked God he was completely free from sexual temptation. I told Kevin he was on very dangerous ground. There is no human being alive who is free from ever being tempted.

The Bible says, "If you think you are standing firm, be careful that you don't fall!" (1 Cor 10:12). And it is true. We are all capable of being tempted and falling, and failure to admit that means we are not properly guarding our steps. We must be honest. If we have a weakness, then we should not put ourselves in positions where we will be tempted to give in to it. If I don't want ice cream, I should not order it and then have to sit staring at it. If I don't want to spend my time slandering others, then I should not develop close relationships with those who do so.

On occasion I have to walk through the red light district alone. I don't like doing this, but there are times when it is unavoidable. So I have worked out a route that does not pass any of the prostitutes or sex shops. It takes me a little longer, but I do not want to present my mind with avoidable temptations.

If we are to give no opportunity to the flesh, then why do I live in the red light district at all? God has called my wife and me to this city and to this neighborhood. If we must be in a place where temptation is strong, then we should only be there at God's direction and in his strength. Occasionally all of us will find ourselves in compromising positions that could present temptation to sin. However, we must make very sure that these situations are not of our instigation or willful choosing and then we take the steps necessary to avoid sin.

There are some people who become very concerned when, after renouncing their sin and walking in the victory Jesus brings, they still feel prone to the sins that formally had power over them. I like to look at it as a desert in which there are rutted creek beds which are often dry for years at a time. When rain comes, the water rushes into the ruts of the creek beds it has carved out over the years and flows along.

Our minds are like those creek beds. We get into the habit of thinking and reacting in certain ways. When we totally give ourselves to Christ, the driving force to think and do ungodly things is removed. The power that once held us in those habitual ruts has been broken, but the ruts are sometimes still there. Those old sin patterns are the ones most likely to trip us up, and are the easiest to fall back into. The good news, however, is that Christ has freed us from the power those patterns once exerted over us. As we grow in Christ, those old ruts also will also be washed away! But meanwhile, we have to be alert to those sins and never get so sure of ourselves that we begin to believe we could never fall into the same ones again.

To lead righteous lives we all need the power of Christ, but failure to admit we are weak will lead to our not claiming his strength. The victorious Christian life is not meant to be lived on the edge of a steep cliff face, clinging on by our fingertips lest we fall. We should live as far from the edge of temptation as we can possibly get!

For leaders in high-profile ministries it is tempting to cover sin, override accountability and put oneself above the need to be open and honest. Christians encourage this type of action by treating spiritual leaders as if they are able to do no wrong.

There have been some Christian leaders who have not successfully protected themselves from temptation. They have not walked in openness and honesty, leading to some tragic results when it was all suddenly exposed. The secular media loves it when the sordid facts are uncovered.

How different this could be if those involved would be open and honest. Instead of a "Christian family matter" being worked out between those concerned, the whole North American public has been treated to scandals which brought shame and embarrassment to all Christians.

No Magic Formula

There is no pat formula that guarantees we will always succeed in enjoying Christ's lordship over every sin. In fact, there are no secrets to overcoming sin. Yet over the centuries and still today, people enter into and enjoy that life. God never intended Christians to live constantly in the quagmire of personal struggle with sin. We must recognize, however, that the potential for sin is resident within us and overcoming sin is one of the chief ways in which we grow and mature in the Christian life.

The apparent paradox here soon dissolves when we understand that it is not just the presence of sin but how we respond to it that is crucial for victory. We must bring any known sin to Jesus, realizing that there is no sin and no amount of sin he cannot forgive if we come to him in sincerity. If we continue to struggle on and on with one particular sin and never make any headway, then something is wrong. You may need to seek help from a godly counselor or a Christian psychologist. There are many such people who love the Lord Jesus and would agree with the principles that are outlined here. Asking for help is not a sign of weakness but of maturity.

We are told nowhere in Scripture that we will enjoy sinless life, but that we can enjoy victorious Christian life. If you go through a difficulty with sin and you bring it to the Lord, and you gain victory over that sin so that it is no longer dominating you, you are enjoying victorious Christian life. If, however, you are making no headway in your struggle and are constantly falling back into personal sin, read this book again, praying over the principles in it and asking God for help to put them into practice.

There are no secrets or magic formulas for overcoming sin, but there are biblical principles that need to be obeyed. And there is wonderful provision of victory over sin through the death of the Lord on the cross. As we accept his victory and abide in it, then we will know his resurrection power in our lives.

Earlier I said we matured through overcoming sin. And that is true. But at the same time we must also stop struggling and rely on God's power. We must come to such an assurance of his love for us and of our ultimate triumph because of what he has done for us on the cross. Paul encouraged Philippian Christians to be "confident of this, that he who began a good work in you will carry it on to completion until the day of Christ Jesus" (Phil 1:6). As we rest in faith, actively trusting the Lord Jesus, we enable the Holy Spirit to work deep in our hearts.

Stop struggling, dear Christian friend, and turn to Jesus for he alone is the victor. He has conquered sin, death, hell, the grave and all the forces of evil. Give all your worries and failures to the Lord Jesus. Worship him and receive from him mercy and forgiveness and hope. Rest in his unfailing love.

If your heart condemns you, remember that "God is greater than your heart." He is greater than any sin. Do not try to do something to atone for your past failures or to try and earn his love. He loves you because he loves you. Accept that fact right now; take time even now to accept his love.

Allow God to reveal to you how sin disappoints and grieves him. Sin in our lives brings great disappointment to God. He is a holy God. Sin is totally contrary to his nature of purity, truthfulness and goodness. Ask God to reveal to you his grief over your sin.

Respond to his love out of gratitude. Obey him, but let your acts of obedience be love-responses to his great kindness and mercy. May I suggest you pray with me right now?

Dear Father,

Thank you for your wonderful love for me; I can't repay it, Father, but I want to tell you how grateful I am. Forgive me, Father, for sinning against you. Cleanse me from all unrighteousness. I turn from my sin now, by your strength and through your grace. Amen.

Questions for Individuals or Groups

1. Why is it hard to be honest with God?

2. How can consciously bringing sinful thoughts to God help us?

3. How can confessing sins to another Christian also help us combat those sins (pp. 88-90)?

4. Why is fleeing temptation a common sense strategy for handling our weaknesses (pp. 90-94)?

5. What are some practical steps you could take to make sure you don't put yourself in the way of temptation?

6. Comment on McClung's statement, "Asking for help is not a sign of weakness but of maturity" (p. 95).

7. The author notes that overcoming sin involves both resisting sin and overcoming sin, relying instead on God (p. 95). How are both true?

Eight

Power to
Turn Away
from Sin

REPENTANCE. Is it merely a feeling of remorse that sweeps over us? Or wishing we hadn't done something that backfired on us? When do we know we have truly repented?

We are told in 2 Corinthians 7:10 about a godly sorrow and a worldly sorrow. Godly sorrow is repentance; worldly sorrow is regret. Repentance implies that if we had the opportunity to commit that sin again we would not. Regret, on the other hand, suggests that we would do it again, but in such a way as to try to avoid the consequences.

I'm sure many prisoners in jails regret committing the crime that led to their imprisonment, yet given the chance, they probably would commit that crime again. Some prisoners spend months, even years, plotting the "perfect crime." They have no intention of giving up their criminal lifestyle—they only want to avoid the consequences.

Or consider an unmarried couple who is sexually involved. If the woman gets pregnant, they may either regret not taking proper precautions or repent of having had sex outside of marriage. Repentance means that we see the intrinsic wrong of our sin. The outworking of this is that when confronted with the same temptation another time, we will say no. Regret is only sorrow about not covering our tracks.

Brokenhearted God

True repentance occurs when we begin to see sin from God's point of view—when we see the way our sin has broken his heart. Perhaps the idea that God's heart can be broken by our sin is new to you. In Genesis 6:5-6 we are told, "Then the LORD saw that the wickedness of man was great on the earth, and that every intent of the thoughts of his heart was only evil continually. And the LORD was sorry that he had made man on the earth, and he was grieved in his heart" (NASB). God was so disappointed with what he saw that there was a grief or sorrow in his heart.

Jesus also was brokenhearted as he wept over Jerusalem. "O Jerusalem, Jerusalem, you who kill the prophets and stone those sent to you, how often I have longed to gather your children together, as a hen gathers her chicks under her wings, but you were not willing!" (Lk 13:34). God's heart aches over our sin. It alienates us from him and from our fellow believers.

If we want to have victory over sin and turn our lives wholeheartedly over to God, then we must see our sin from God's perspective. No sermon on hell can ever change a person's heart like seeing the grief sin has brought to the heart of the One who created us. We must ask God to show us what our sin does to him. As we do this and begin to understand his great love for us, despite how much we have hurt him and grieved his heart, turning away from that sin is the natural thing to do. This is the test of our sincerity and of the level of our desperation to be right with God.

The Holy Spirit is continually at work in our hearts to help us respond in this manner. Paul asks in Romans 2:4, "Do you show contempt for the riches of his kindness, tolerance and patience, not realizing that God's kindness leads you toward repentance?"

I remember how hurt I was when I realized my daughter Misha, who was six years old at the time, was lying to me. Sally and I had read in several childrearing books that most children go through stages like this, and the authors of these books suggested we demonstrate to our child the importance of telling the truth.

We tried every way we could think of to do this. We discussed it with her, spanked her, took away privileges and encouraged her when she told the truth. But all was to no avail. Her lying got worse.

Eventually, out of desperation, we stopped everything and started to pray. (Parents as well as children can be slow learners!) One morning soon after that I felt the Lord say, "Take Misha for a walk before she goes off to school."

When we had walked some distance from the house, I stopped and knelt down so I could look her in the eyes. Very gently I said, "Misha, I just can't trust you any more." Tears began to roll down my cheeks as I continued: "It hurts Daddy so much that he can't trust his daughter. What are we going to do about it?"

She was taken by surprise at my tears. She had seen us threaten, spank and reprimand, but never cry over the situation. Her little face grimaced in sorrow, and I could see that for the first time she understood that her sin was affecting me and our relationship. I didn't say any more, and we arranged to meet in my office after school.

Sally and I were waiting for her in my office when she arrived home from school. I repeated the question, "Misha, what are we going to do?"

She walked over to me and began to cry. "Daddy, what can I do so you will trust me again?" She threw her arms around me and sobbed, "Daddy, I'm sorry. Please forgive me. I don't want to hurt you."

Sally and I began to weep with her, and I said, "Misha, we forgive you." After I had said those words, something changed in the situation. Trust for Misha returned to my heart. That was not the first time she had apologized for lying to me, but I knew that this time she had had a revelation of how much her sin hurt me. In her six-year-old heart she truly repented that day. I forgave her and trust was restored. From that time on her pattern of lying was broken. God's heart breaks for us in the same way, and he deeply desires that our relationship with him be restored.

Reveal Your Heart

I want to challenge you to be very serious with God at this point. It is absolutely essential to set aside time with God—at least an afternoon or evening—where you can ask him to show you your heart from his perspective. A prayer like the one below is a good starting point:

Dear Lord Jesus,

I cannot see or fully understand my heart's motives. I desperately need you to give me a revelation of my heart as you see it. I ask you, Lord Jesus, to come by your Holy Spirit and show me those things in my heart that grieve and displease you. Show me any root of pride or independence, and show me the manifestations of my sinful nature. I need to see how I hurt both you and others.

Protect me from condemnation and introspection. I ask that this will be a work of your Spirit. Show me your love for me as an expression of your holiness and how you long for me to do nothing that would grieve you.

Thank you that you died on the cross to set me free from sin, and that you are praying and interceding for me to live the kind of life that will please you. In Jesus' name I pray.

I remember how Don, the youth leader in a church my father pastored, set aside several days to pray and ask God to reveal how he viewed his heart. At eleven o'clock on the second night there was a loud thump on our door and my father got up to answer it. At the door he found Don weeping. "Pastor McClung, please pray with me," he said. "God has shown me how ugly my heart is!"

My father spent a long time praying with Don that evening. As a result, over the next months Don's whole outlook on life changed. He began caring so much more about others and developed a zeal to win the lost. It was obvious to us all that Don had not merely spent his time in personal contemplation and introspection—he had truly met with God.

Claim Victory

Each of us needs to see our sin from God's viewpoint, but we also need to go on and claim the victory and joy he has for us as we overcome. God doesn't want us to remain stuck in a state of deeply felt guilt. That would be to miss the whole purpose of repentance—entering into victorious Christian living. After God has shown you his grief and sorrow over sin, ask him for his forgiveness and receive it by faith, fully committed to turning away from those things that have grieved the Lord.

And if you sin again, come back to the Lord again. If the thought comes into your mind, "You have failed. You can never make it. You are nothing but a hypocrite," agree in principle but do not accept that there is no hope. Each time you fall, come back to the Lord. Let your weakness drive you back to the Lord Jesus.

The enemy wants to use our failures to keep us away from the Lord, but don't give in to his lies. I find it helpful to say to the enemy or myself or whoever says I've blown it, "You're right, and I accept responsibility for it. I've failed again, but I bring it to Jesus." Then, take it to God:

Lord,

I'm sorry. Please forgive me. This really discourages me, but I refuse to let this come between you and me, Lord. I choose to be sincere even though I feel like a terrible failure. You are the only one who can really help me and forgive me, Lord. I receive your forgiveness because of the promise in your Word to forgive me any time I come to you and confess my sin.

The promise of forgiveness is found in 1 John 1:9: "If we confess our sins, he is faithful and just and will forgive us our sins and purify us from all unrighteousness." I suggest you memorize this verse right now if you have not done so already.

The Fruit of Repentance
There are times when God may prompt us to go and confess to and ask forgiveness of those we have sinned against. He may also ask us to make restitution to these people. Sometimes it can be confusing to know exactly who to go to, and we must listen closely to the voice of the Spirit. As a general rule, though, we should go to those directly affected by our sin.

If it is between you and God, then go to him in prayer. If you have had a poor attitude which has caused tension at work, then go to your boss or to those coworkers your attitude has directly affected. If, on the other hand, you have had impure thoughts toward another person and they are unaware of it, then it is a matter between you and God. To go to that person and confess your sin in this instance can often cause unnecessary damage to the person and to your relationship with them.

True repentance occurs when we see what grief our sin has brought to God's heart and when we determine that we will not, even if we find ourselves in the same circumstances, commit that sin again. However, our motive for not committing that sin again should not be the pain and grief it will bring us, but because of the pain and grief it will bring to God's heart.

The Refining Fire
Many years ago I came to a crisis point in my relationship with others. I had hurt several close friends deeply, shown disrespect for my wife, and was struggling with my relationship with God. I went for a walk one day in the forest. I decided to put my life

totally on the line for the Lord. I knew at that point it had to be all or nothing. No superficial response could deal with the crisis I had created for myself.

I confessed my predicament to the Lord, acknowledged my sin, and then prayed a prayer that went something like this:

Lord, I desperately need you in my life. I choose not to go around this situation. I ask you to use this time in my life to bring me to a place of brokenness. Do anything you need to do in my life to produce humility and Christlikeness in me.

I ask you to be ruthless in dealing with my sin. No matter how long it takes, Lord, or what you have to do, I welcome your loving judgment in my heart. Expose anything and everything in my life you want to.

No matter what the cost, Lord, I commit myself to your way. I refuse to push myself forward or to avoid your dealing in my character. I ask for there to be no shortcuts to my growth. If it takes ten, fifteen or twenty years, I say yes to you, Lord.

It was at that point that God really began to work in my character. I invited his refining fire no matter how hot it got! I asked for his bright light of truth to be turned upon my heart no matter what was shown to be there and no matter who found out. I asked God to produce brokenness in me no matter how long it took. I committed myself to be ruthless with my sin. I decided to take the attitude that in every conflict I had from that point on with others, I would believe God wanted to use that conflict to show what was in my heart.

As L. E. Maxwell says in his book *Born Crucified:*

Many people wonder why they have no victory over their wounded pride, their touchiness, their greediness . . . the secret is not far away. They secretly and habitually practice shrine worship—at the shrine of self. In the outward cross they glory but inwardly they worship another god and stretch out their hands to serve a pitied, petty, and pampered selflife. Until Christ works out in you an inner crucifixion which will cut you off from self-infatuation and unite you to God in a deep union of love, a thousand heavens could not give you peace.[1]

I ask you today, right now, to make that same commitment I made years ago and still believe with all my heart. I cannot express to you how glad I am that I have chosen God's way. God has been faithful to me, and I rejoice that he has answered my prayer!

Questions for Individuals or Groups

1. How does the author contrast repentance with regret (pp. 97-98)?

2. What do you think it means for God to be brokenhearted by our sin (pp. 98-100)?

3. Why is it important to see our sin from God's viewpoint?

4. How can our failures drive us away from God or bring us closer to him (p. 102)?

5. Why should we go to those who have been affected by our sin to restore the relationship or to make restitution?

6. What are some situations or relationships you might need to clear up? What action should you take?

7. Why would it be inappropriate to confess to someone you have had lustful thoughts about (p. 103)?

8. Take time to memorize 1 John 1:9.

Note

[1] L. E. Maxwell, *Born Crucified* (Chicago: Moody Press, 1984).

Nine

Pride:
The Unseen
Sin

THERE are seven deadly sins, and pride leads the list:

> There are six things the LORD hates, seven that are detestable to him: haughty eyes, a lying tongue, hands that shed innocent blood, a heart that devises wicked schemes, feet that are quick to rush into evil, a false witness who pours out lies and a man who stirs up dissension among brothers. (Prov 6:16-19)

Pride is no respecter of persons. Its victims are old and young, rich and poor, ordained and layperson. It camouflages itself in many subtle forms, but when its work is done, the telltale marks of alienation, jealousy, hatred and disloyalty are left behind.

What Is Pride?

Pride is an undue sense of one's own superiority and inordinate self-esteem. It is arrogance and conceit. It is raising ourselves above others. It is extreme self-centeredness. It is pretending to be something we are not. It is refusal to acknowledge our weaknesses or to recognize our natural limitations. It is covering up our problems or sins from those we should be open with. It is hiding behind excuses, rationalizations and defense mechanisms. If it is left undealt with, pride will eventually deceive us and blind us to its working in our life. "The pride of your heart has deceived you" (Obad 3). It is the unseen sin.

Some confusion occurs when we talk of pride. We can talk about being proud of our achievements and abilities, proud of our spouses and proud of our children, but none of these are what the Bible calls *pride*. Indeed, we are admonished by Scripture to have an honest estimation of our abilities and strengths and not be constantly effacing ourselves.

Pride, as defined in the Bible, is something quite different. It is deliberately choosing not to acknowledge and work out God's character and lordship in our lives. Instead, we exalt our way of doing things and say to God: "I'll do this my way. Don't interfere in my life. When I need you, I'll call."

The greatest hindrance to knowing God is pride. The greatest obstacle to loving other people is pride. Every sin committed by humanity can be traced back to pride; every war, every instance of human conflict, every divided family can be traced back to pride.

The Bible speaks in very strong terms about God's attitude toward pride. In Job 35:12 it says that people cry out, and God gives no answer because of their pride. In Proverbs we read:

"The LORD detests all the proud of heart. . . . Pride goes before destruction" (16:5, 18).

Pride is very subtle. The devil does not walk up to you and announce that at three o'clock in the afternoon he is going to hit you with a "pride attack." Pride does not come upon you in a sudden, violent way. It is treacherous.

As C. S. Lewis has written in *Mere Christianity:*

It is pride that has been the chief cause of misery in every nation and family since the world began. Other vices may sometimes bring people together. You may find good fellowship, jokes, and friendliness amongst drunken people or unchaste people, but pride always means enmity. It is enmity not only between man and man, but between man and God. In God you come up against something that is in every respect immeasurably superior to yourself. Unless you know God as that and therefore know yourself as nothing in comparison, you do not know God at all. As long as you are proud, you cannot know God.[1]

I have found it very difficult to discern pride in my own life. It is deceptive. I have desperately needed God and others to help me see the pride that is in my life. I am convinced that God will reveal the pride of our hearts if we ask him.

Are you prepared for such a revelation? God will grant us understanding if we sincerely ask him. He does that to help us, not humiliate us. He sees the destruction and hurt that comes through our pride and therefore wants to set us free from its powerful hold on our minds and hearts.

Where Can Pride Be Found?

Pride will grow wherever the conditions are favorable. While it is easy to have an idealized view of the early church, we must not lose sight of the fact that the writers of the Epistles wrote to some churches to remind them of their potential for pride. "Let us not become conceited, provoking and envying each other," writes Paul to the church in Galatia (Gal 5:26).

Jesus also had to deal with pride in his disciples. James and John thought they had things all worked out. In heaven, one would sit on Jesus' right side, the other on his left. All they wanted was for Jesus to use his "influence" in arranging things with the Father (Mk 10:35-41). However, instead of his cooperation they received a lesson in servanthood. "You know that those who are regarded as rulers of the Gentiles lord it over them, and their high officials exercise authority over them. Not so with you. Instead, whoever wants to be great among you must be your servant" (Mk 10:42-43).

Throughout church history pride has wrought havoc, creating bitterness, division and strife, and we should not assume we are any less immune from it today. To detect pride in our lives we need to look for its outward manifestations—broken relationships and alienation.

The Author of Pride

The Bible is very explicit about who is the author of pride—Satan himself. In the allegorical narrative in Isaiah chapter 14, Satan is recorded as saying about himself: "I will ascend to heaven; I will raise my throne above the stars of God; I will sit enthroned on the mount of assembly, on the utmost heights of the sacred mountain. I will ascend above the tops of the clouds; I will make myself like the Most High" (Is 14:13-14).

Satan's entire emphasis was on the things he thought he could do, but the last claim is perhaps the most revealing—he believed he had the ability to make himself like God. Notice how many times *I* occurs in the passage. Satan scorned dependence on God, choosing instead to use his own wisdom and way of doing things.

Down through the centuries, these same thoughts have been expressed again and again. We have allowed and encouraged pride to grow in our hearts. We continue to believe we can do things without God. We think we can take God's place and steer our lives in any direction we choose. We try to make God a sort of good-luck charm to be called upon in times of personal emergency.

The character of God and pride form opposite ends of the scale. Satan is the author and perfecter of pride, God the author and perfecter of humility. The two cannot coexist. We must decide who we will give our allegiance to and who we will seek to imitate in our attitudes and choices, particularly as we develop relationships in three significant areas of our Christian lives.

Pride and Our Relationship to God

We are God's creation. He intricately designed and brought each of us into being. He knows all there is to know about us.

In every way, God is vastly superior to his creation. He is infinite; we are finite. He is righteous; we all have sinned and are unrighteous. He is wise; we are foolish. He is ever the same; we are constantly changing. Those who refuse to honor God, who deny him or underestimate his power, err to the point of ludicrousness. If we fail to see God as immeasurably superior to ourselves, we fail to see him at all. In confining him to our limited concepts we, in essence, deny him and all he has done.

In order to have a relationship with God we must first acknowledge his vastly superior wisdom, strength and knowledge.
Pride will paralyze our ability to do this. But if we fail to do
it, we will eventually be cut off completely from God. This may
seem harsh. "Surely," we reason, "a little pride will not hurt.
After all, nobody is perfect."

The Bible, however, allows no such concession to this deadly
sin. God is merciful, but the Bible speaks unequivocally about
God's reaction to pride. Pride is an abomination to him (Prov
16:5, 18) and he will not tolerate it. Pride will only hurt our
relationship with God. The Bible says God goes out of his way
to oppose and resist the proud person (Jas 4:6).

Faced with this, we have two choices. Either we cooperate
with God and ask for his help in eliminating pride from our
lives, or we face alienation and separation from our Maker
forever. As we move on and look more closely at the root of
pride and the destruction it brings in the next chapter, we will
begin to understand why pride is such an abomination to God.

We need God on our side. We need his strength and wisdom.
We need his grace and redeeming power. To alienate ourselves
from him is the most foolish thing we could ever do. God opposes the proud, but gives grace to the humble. We must be
certain we're in the camp of the humble and enjoying God's
grace.

Pride and Our Relationship to Others

Pride also alienates us from others. If we judge others, if we
deem them to be either inferior or superior, then it will affect
our relationships. If we think a person is inferior, then we feel
justified in putting them down. If on the other hand we think

them superior, we are the ones who feel put down and unworthy. In this situation our pride turns on us, enslaving us in a preoccupation with what others think.

The greatest obstacle in loving other people is pride. We all make mistakes, and sometimes another's mistake may leave us feeling hurt or depressed—we may even want to deliberately hurt them back. At this point we are faced with a choice: We can repent of our bitterness, forgive the person for what they have done to us and set the matter right, or we can continue on the path we have set for ourselves—a path that leads straight to destruction. Forgiving a person who has hurt us frees us from the bondage of bitterness and allows us to grow emotionally and spiritually.

Pride cripples our ability to get along with others and leaves us isolated and alone. It wrecks relationships, setting husband against wife, parent against child, friend against friend, and leaves us with our hurt which, if left unchecked, will harden into hatred and alienation.

Proud Christians also divide churches. They murmur against their leaders, judge their fellow believers, and actively promote division. Not only do they alienate themselves and their church, but they also alienate those who look to the body of Christ as an example of unity in action.

Pride and Ourselves

Not only does pride destroy our relationships with God and others, but it also wreaks havoc in our own lives. Proverbs 26:12 tells us there is one thing worse than a fool and that is a proud man. Indeed, a proud man is the biggest fool of all because his pride will bring him low, leading to his ultimate destruction (Prov 29:23).

A teachable spirit and a willingness to learn quickly from others is the greatest protection there is from the consequences of other people's sins against us. As strange as it may seem, the greatest release from hurt, rejection and emotional damage other people force upon us is to walk in humility. It protects us from problems that we otherwise have no control over.

We desperately need God. The most foolish and self-destructive thing we could ever do is to alienate ourselves from him. God longs to help us. That is why he sent his Son to die for us. It is his love that reaches out to us to heal us and deliver us from our fear, pride and the walls they bring between us and others.

Many times in my life I have had to rely on others for help in recognizing my own pride. If you pray for God to reveal pride to you, don't be surprised if others start exhorting you about weaknesses in your life. When confronted, it is not always easy to admit we are wrong. But, if we are to enjoy the blessing of humility, it is imperative.

My wife, Sally, and I have sometimes disagreed about how we should discipline our children. When disagreements arose, we would immediately take sides and argue. Attitudes would harden, and before long all sorts of other issues were dragged into the disagreement. When this happened, my objective shifted from what was best for the children to proving, at any cost, that I was right. After one such encounter, Sally told me she felt I was allowing this to make me judgmental and proud. My focus was no longer on what was best for the family, but on getting my own way. It was hard to admit at first, but she was right.

God's intention in revealing pride in our lives is always for our benefit. He wants to help, not humiliate us. Through generation after generation, God, with great sadness in his heart, has seen destruction wrought by pride. He longs for us to be freed of it by taking the crucial step of asking him to reveal the pride lurking in our hearts.

Questions for Individuals or Groups

1. What do we normally mean by the word *pride?*

2. McClung writes that pride is "deliberately choosing not to acknowledge and work out God's character and lordship in our lives" (p. 108). How do you respond to this? Explain.

3. How was pride at the core of Satan's rebellion against God (pp. 110-11)?

4. What are some of the ways pride has affected your relationship with God (pp. 111-12)?

5. Why do you think that God has such an intensely negative reaction to pride?

6. How does pride alienate us from other people (pp. 112-13)?

7. How has it affected your relationships with people?

8. What are the ways pride can affect us personally (pp. 113-15)?

9. Why does Proverbs 26:12 suggest that one thing worse than a fool is a proud man?

Note

[1] C. S. Lewis, *Mere Christianity* (New York: Macmillian, 1964).

Ten

How to See
the Unseeable

THE symptoms of pride can be likened to those of cancer. At first we're unaware of it, and it grows unnoticed. Slowly, we become aware that something is not functioning as it should be. A leg aches, we feel nauseated, or a lump begins growing on a cheek. Now we are faced with two choices: go to a doctor for diagnosis and treatment, or pretend nothing is wrong. In the early stages it is easy to hide the symptoms, but as time goes by, it becomes more and more difficult. We can no longer walk without an exaggerated limp, face eating a meal or talk because of the pain in our cheek. The growth which started out so insignificant has become a consuming and potentially fatal illness.

So it is with pride. At first the symptoms are almost unnoticeable—we become a little impatient when inconvenienced; we avoid certain people; it takes a little longer than before to forgive someone; we struggle to say "You're right, I'm wrong" when corrected. Again we have two choices: ignore these symptoms as insignificant, or go to God and ask him to show us the extent of the problem and help us deal with it. If we ignore pride, rest assured, it will continue to multiply until everyone can see the cancerous pride we have allowed to consume us.

Jesus once said, "By their fruit you will recognize them" (Mt 7:16). Let's look more closely at the fruit of pride. Each of the following sections begins with Scripture, describes a fruit of pride and concludes with a prayer. Don't rush past this chapter. You may want to meditate and pray through it one section a day. I suggest going through it on your knees, asking God to do a deep, radical and life-changing work in your heart.

Stealing from God

"I am the Lord; that is my name! I will not give my glory to another or my praise to idols" (Is 42:8).

Each of us has gifts and abilities that God has placed within us. These range from a beautiful singing voice to organizational abilities to being able to grow a magnificent garden. And, an honest estimation of our gifts is necessary if we are to develop the talents God has invested in us. However, it is a dangerous form of pride that causes us to take credit for the gifts God has given us. By giving the impression that we are in some way responsible for these gifts, we take the credit away from God, and he emphatically states, "I will not give My glory to another." Taking credit for the good God has enabled us to do is stealing from God.

Dear Lord, Everything good in my life is from you. You have invested many gifts and abilities into my life. Help me to use them for your glory. Help me to serve you graciously, continually working for you and your kingdom. I do not want to start out in your name and finish in mine, taking the credit for what you have done in and through me. Keep me walking close to you. Show me any way I have stolen your glory as I wait now in silence before you.

Self-Centeredness

"As each one has received a special gift, employ it in serving one another" (1 Pet 4:10).

Within Christianity there are those who use a façade of spirituality to cover their inward selfishness. If, in the exercising of our gifts, we overlook the feelings of others, then we need to re-examine our "gift." If we are not using our abilities to bring blessing to others, then we are misusing the abilities God has given us.

Self-centered pride feeds a desire to be served, to be right, to be noticed and to have wishes catered to. It says: "Do it my way," "My ministry," "My vision," "My plan." The underlying assumption here is, "I deserve this because I have earned it."

How shallow this is compared to Paul's response to the Corinthians, "So I will very gladly spend for you everything I have and expend myself as well" (2 Cor 12:15). Paul exemplifies the attitude we should have in serving others. When we can gladly be spent in the service of others without any concern as to how others should serve us, then we have become free from the bondage of self-centeredness.

I have good news for you: God does not want to hurt our

pride . . . he wants to kill it! Only through a deathblow at the heart of our egotism and self-centeredness can we become the people God created us to be.

Dear Lord, So often when I am asked to do things for others my first response is, "What will I get out it?" Teach me how to spend myself for others, to submerge myself in your will, so that my own preferences become secondary to completing the task you have called me to. Face me with myself when I am self-centered. Allow me to see myself as you see me and grant me the courage to look to you and be changed.

Demanding Spirit

"I know what it is to be in need, and I know what it is to have plenty. I have learned the secret of being content in any and every situation, whether well fed or hungry, whether living in plenty or in want" (Phil 4:12).

The pride which is in demanding hearts is revealed because they constantly bring attention to the things that have not been done for them, rather than the things that have been done for them. In demanding that people do things their way, they are in essence saying, "I am superior to you." They are always looking out for their rights. They feel entitled to what they deserve, quite oblivious to the fact that all of us deserve eternal separation from God.

Those who have seen the pride that inhabits their hearts and have cried out in repentance and asked for forgiveness from it know only a deep sense of unworthiness at receiving anything better than that which they deserve. They realize that everything outside of hell is grace. We must never forget we have already received the greatest gift of all—Jesus.

Dear Lord, How often I look at what should be done for me. If someone breaks a promise or fails to live up to what they have agreed upon, I become angry. I think, "Surely I deserve more than this." But I can see from your word that I really do not deserve anything. I have no right to demand my way.

Show me when I am demanding of others, or even of you. Reveal all the ungratefulness in my heart. Replace my demanding heart with gratefulness for all you have done for me.

Superiority

"Be of the same mind toward one another; do not be haughty in mind, but associate with the lowly. Do not be wise in your own estimation" (Rom 12:16 NASB).

Pride causes us to feel we are more important than others. We act haughtily, in a manner revealing an inner attitude of condescension, a belief that somehow we are closer to God or just better than other people. But the Bible teaches that each of us is a sinner, desperately in need of the Lord and others. It is pride, not doctrines or disagreements, which separates us. Our pride tells us we have more truth and therefore are more spiritual than other people. If only we truly believed in our hearts that we each had something to give and receive from one another, then disunity, church divisions, mistrust, conflict and disagreement would evaporate.

Do you look down on people who have not had your spiritual experience, who are from another ethnic group, denomination, age group or are members of the opposite sex? Are there people of certain theological persuasions whom you look upon as less spiritual than yourself? Are there Christians you are uncomfortable fellowshiping with simply because of their beliefs or spiritual gifts? By refusing to associate with some Christians, we reveal the pride in our hearts.

Do you value some people more than others? Are you partial to the rich? Is a refugee less important than an accountant? If we each cost God the same price, dare we think we are any more worthy than others?

I once commented to a friend that I would not associate with a certain group of Christians because of their aberrant theology. They were doing more harm than good. I conceded that they were indeed Christians, but I felt that they should be avoided at all costs.

My friend challenged this attitude. She did not defend their beliefs, but she pointed out that my attitudes and actions were not Christlike and rooted in pride. As I prayed about my friend's exhortations, I began to see that the greater problem was not the poor theology of those I disagreed with, but my own arrogance. I was disassociating myself from those Christ gave his name to, those he had adopted and brought close to himself (Eph 2:14).

Dear Lord, Thank you that you were an example to us of servanthood. You did not consider equality with God something to be grasped, but humbled yourself and took the form of a servant. I too want to humble myself. Rid me of my tendency to show partiality. Free me from racism of any kind. Deliver me from the bondage of superiority so that I may be truly useful in your kingdom. Help me to encourage those around me and serve others with an open heart, wanting the best for their lives. Forgive me for avoiding certain Christians and for thinking I was more spiritual. I repent of these sins in Jesus' name.

Sarcasm

"No man can tame the tongue. It is a restless evil, full of deadly poison. . . . But if you harbor bitter envy and selfish ambition in your hearts, do not boast about it or deny the truth" (Jas 3:8, 14).

Caustic comments may be socially acceptable, but they have no place in the kingdom of God. Sarcasm is a thinly veiled attempt to impress people by highlighting the faults of others. Its humor is always at the expense of another person. Using sarcasm sometimes reveals that we have been hurt or offended by others and have not had the courage to deal with it openly. Instead, we allowed bitterness to grow in our hearts.

Jesus never used sarcasm when dealing with his disciples. When a problem arose, he spoke directly, not surreptitiously, to the person involved. Let us take his example and deal straightforwardly with issues that have the potential for hurt instead of resorting to sarcasm. And let us repent of all humor that makes people of other races or nationalities the brunt of our jokes.

Dear Lord, When I think of the things I am capable of saying, I realize how much I need your Holy Spirit to purify my speech. How many times I have spoken with no thought to the damage I was doing to those you have told me to love. Lord, I admit I cannot at the same time really love people and make fun of them. Forgive me for sarcasm, Lord Jesus.

Help me to think the best of others, and to use my speech to encourage them and build them up. Refresh my mind with positive things to say about others. Even a fool can see the negative qualities in another, but it takes a wise man to see the positive. Teach me wisdom. Replace my sarcasm with

words of thanks and praise. Give me the courage to ask forgiveness where I have hurt others.

A Critical Attitude

"Do not let any unwholesome talk come out of your mouths,
but only what is helpful for building others up according to
their needs, that it may benefit those who listen. And do not
grieve the Holy Spirit of God, with whom you were sealed for
the day of redemption. Get rid of all bitterness, rage and anger,
brawling and slander, along with every form of malice. Be kind
and compassionate to one another, forgiving each other, just as
in Christ God forgave you" (Eph 4:29-32).

Proud people are critical and judgmental. They have difficulty seeing the good in others and are quick to negate the
positive through a critical approach. In judging another person
we are actually saying, "I can do better. Why don't they just
move over and let me do it?"

Ephesians 4:29-32 implies a number of things about critical
speech. First, when we speak against a fellow Christian we
speak against and grieve the Holy Spirit. Second, slander, gossip and negative speech are divisive and destructive. Third, we
are to speak only those things that build others up. We must
never forget that one day we will give an account to God for
every word we have spoken.

Critical people have difficulty extending grace to others. Paul
declares in Romans 6:14, "For sin shall not be your master,
because you are not under law, but under grace." While we are
grateful to be under God's grace, it is easy to try and put others
under the bondage of our "laws." We must extend the same
grace to others as God has extended to us.

Do you speak about others' faults? Do you derive secret enjoyment from hearing bad news about others? You don't have to lie to slander someone. Just speaking the truth about people's weaknesses can slander them.

Over and over the Lord has convicted me of speaking critical and unkind words. I have found the best way to deal with the situation is to confess the sin to God and to the brother or sister I have spoken against. Be open to God's Spirit and let him reveal any sin you may have in this area.

Dear Lord, How often I have looked down on others. I am quick to judge them without knowing all the facts, and my flesh enjoys building itself up by dwelling on other's shortcomings and problems. Help me to see the good in others, to appreciate their uniqueness instead of wishing everyone was like me. I have often deceived myself, Lord, thinking I was concerned for others when my critical speech was really a sin. God, I ask you to forgive me for spreading mistrust through my critical speech.

Impatience

"Love is patient, love is kind, and is not jealous; love does not brag and is not arrogant, does not act unbecomingly; it does not seek its own, is not provoked, does not take into account a wrong suffered" (1 Cor 13:4-5 NASB).

A friend of mine took a group of Christians on a tour of Europe. The women in the group were perpetually late in arriving back from their shopping expeditions and visits to museums, which annoyed the tour leader intensely. On one particular day he paced back and forth in front of the bus waiting for three overdue ladies to return. Another member of the tour approached him, and whispered in his ear: "Please don't get impatient with them. There's probably a good explanation." Infuriated, he said to her, in full hearing of the tour group, "I've got more patience than you give me credit for!"

By being impatient we are signifying that our ideas, projects, programs and schedules are more important than people. When they fail, we justify our lack of love and self-control and express it through impatience. In the course of a week there are numerous times when we have to wait for others, but becoming impatient at such times, regardless of whether it is the other person's fault or not, is never justified. Instead, we should make such instances opportunities to check the attitudes of our hearts. The other person may be at fault, but we are responsible for the way we react to them.

What do we do if a person has kept us waiting for an hour, or we have had to explain something to them for the third time simply because they didn't consider it important enough to listen the first two times? The answer is simple. We must forgive them, not once, not twice, but as many times as we have to.

I have found I'm most impatient when I think I'm right. I want to forge ahead with implementing my ideas and sometimes fail to see the value of listening to the suggestions of others. As I've worked at listening to others and evaluating their suggestions, I have discovered how valuable their input is. People are not always trying to be obstinate or critical when they admonish us; on the contrary, from their perspective they are able to see things that I cannot see. Out of love they want to share their concerns with me so that I can avoid any unnecessary embarrassment, failure or frustration.

Dear Lord, You have been so patient with me. You have

extended your grace and forgiveness to me so many times. When I think of what you have done for me, what you ask me to do for others seems little in comparison. Convict me when I fail to offer that same patience and love to those around me. Stop me every time I am impatient in my heart. Convict me when I am slow to forgive, and show me the level of holiness you have set for me in this area of my life.

Envy and Greed

"Watch out! Be on your guard against all kinds of greed; a man's life does not consist in the abundance of his possessions" (Lk 12:15).

Envy and greed stem from a belief that we have a right to more than we presently have. There is some erroneous teaching in the church today which suggests material wealth is synonymous with God's blessing. As a result, some Christians are busy amassing money and possessions to prove how righteous and spiritual they are—how much they enjoy God's favor. Yet, even a cursory reading of the New Testament reveals that the disciples did not grow rich and prosperous after Jesus' death. Were they unspiritual? Nowhere does the New Testament teach that money and possessions are a sign of God's approval.

Jesus explicitly tells us not to put our trust in material things. If he had to warn people of his day to beware of being overcome by greed and covetousness, how much more should *we* be on guard! Greed will fill our hearts with longings for more—more money and more possessions. Instead of focusing on and being content with what we have, we will constantly be lusting after those things we do not have.

Greed is a way of looking at the world that has little to do with what we actually have. I have seen beggars on the streets of Bombay who were more generous with the little they had than some middle-class Christians in prosperous countries. Our lack of generosity infects our spirits and robs us of our hunger for spiritual reality. Our love for evangelism, for studying God's Word and for prayer soon grows dull in a heart consumed by greed.

Dear Lord, Everything I have is from you. The things of this world do not last. Tomorrow everything I own could be gone, so while some put their trust in material things, I will put my trust in you. Help me to set my mind on things of eternal value and see them the way you do. Thank you for all you have provided for me and help me, in your name, to reach out and provide for those in need. May I never reject what you have called me to do because of an unwillingness to make the material sacrifices involved. I repent of attitudes of greed, and I turn from acts of conspicuous consumption in a world filled with need. Even though I have failed in the past, today I choose to put your kingdom above all else in my life.

Lack of Forgiveness

"Bless those who persecute you; bless and do not curse. Rejoice with those who rejoice; mourn with those who mourn" (Rom 12:14-15).

As Christians, we are called to weep with those who weep and laugh with those who laugh. Hardhearted people more often find themselves secretly rejoicing when things don't go well for others. They are aloof and unable to comfort and encourage others or rejoice with them in their blessings. They cannot express affection or tenderness.

If, after being persecuted and rejected by someone, we do not make a conscious effort to forgive them and set the matter straight, we are in danger of becoming hardhearted. In that state it is easy to rationalize our bitterness and hostility by focusing on the injustice done to us. At first we think we can control our hardheartedness by focusing it only on the person who has hurt us. But, once we have started down this path, we discover it cannot be applied selectively. Our whole life is soon consumed by bitterness, and we are transformed into resentful people.

The only cure for hardheartedness is to have our hard heart taken out and replaced with the new heart God wants to give us. "I will give you a new heart and put a new spirit in you; I will remove from you your heart of stone and give you a heart of flesh" (Ezek 36:26). How does this happen? Through confessing the state of our hearts, repenting, crying out to the Lord to change us and sharing our need with others.

Forgiveness is a powerful force. Try reading through the New Testament, taking note of every parable, teaching and admonition that deals with forgiveness. You will find there are few books that do not refer to forgiveness. Without God's forgiveness of us, and our subsequent forgiveness of others, there would be no gospel message. Through forgiving those who sin against us, we find new freedom in our hearts.

Dear Lord, My heart is hard. I am quick to judge others and quick to think it serves them right when things go wrong. Sometimes I secretly hope things do not go well for others. I bow before you today and ask for surgery. Take away my hard heart and replace it with the new heart you promise to give. I desperately need you Lord. Break my heart in any way you choose. Teach me to respond to others as you do. Show me how to extend mercy and forgiveness to them. I want to be changed to become more like you.

You taught us to pray, "Forgive us our trespasses as we forgive those who trespass against us." How often I have not been quick to forgive. I have fallen prey to gossip, judging others and rebellion. I know this hurts you, Lord, and works against building your kingdom here on earth. You stand by me in spite of all the mistakes I make, in spite of all the times I have let you down. Give me the grace and strength to do the same for others.

An Unteachable Spirit

"Yet they did not obey or incline their ear, but walked in their own counsels and in the stubbornness of their evil heart, and went backward and not forward" (Jer 7:24 NASB).

None of us is above the need for correction in some area of our lives. When confronted by someone, do you listen or do you ignore what they have to say? Do you accept their reproof or become resentful that they would dare to correct you? Do you rationalize, excuse or explain? Do you find it difficult to say "I am wrong"?

The more mature we become in the Lord, the more we welcome the input and correction of others. In laying aside our pride we benefit from the insights of many wise and godly people. If, however, we are unwilling to accept this kind of input, then we have become unteachable.

Darlene Cunningham, wife of the founder of Youth With A Mission and a close friend, has been an inspiration to me in this area. If a person comes to her with a reproof, she listens without defending herself. When they have finished, she thanks them for caring enough to confront her about what they see as a weakness in her life. She tells them she will pray about what they've said and get back to them. Darlene does not accept every negative thing a person says to her, but she does promise to seek God's perspective on it. When she has done that, she gets back to the person and reports what the Lord has shown her and makes amends for the situation if that is necessary.

In the majority of instances, when we are corrected by someone, there is at least some element of truth in what the person says. By refusing to consider what they have said, or by reacting negatively to them, we miss out on what God wants to teach us. Even if we feel the reprover's motives are suspect or that they also have areas of weakness, we must not lose sight of the fact that truth is truth, regardless of who presents it or how it is presented.

Dear Lord, You know that I am not perfect. I have blind spots in my life. I need others to give me insight into these areas. I want to be a mature and complete Christian, and if that means you will show me my areas of weakness through others, then I will receive what they have to say.

Lord, teach me to come to you when others say things to, or about, me. Help me to search my heart and see if there is truth in what they say, and then strengthen my resolve to deal with the situation in a godly manner. I need your grace in my life to carry this through. Give me grace to say "I am wrong, please forgive me." Lord, help me to learn about you and your ways from every person I meet. Help me to approach every situation with an open and humble spirit.

People-Pleasing

But Samuel replied, "Does the LORD delight in burnt offerings and sacrifices as much as in obeying the voice of the LORD? To obey is better than sacrifice, and to heed is better than the fat of rams. For rebellion is like the sin of divination, and arrogance like the evil of idolatry. Because you have rejected the word of the LORD, he has rejected you as king" (1 Sam 15:22-24).

We can easily become a slave to another person's opinions of us and never enjoy the freedom there is in living to please God. Jesus was confronted one day by a man who wanted to bury his father before making a commitment to Christ. To this man Jesus replied, "Allow the dead to bury their own dead" (Lk 9:60). Now, that does not sound like an attempt to please the relatives! In one of the lesser-quoted beatitudes Jesus also says, "Blessed are you when men hate you, when they exclude you and insult you and reject your name as evil, because of the Son of Man. Rejoice in that day and leap for joy" (Lk 6:22-23).

There are times when we must follow God even if that means not pleasing others. The more ungodly the people around us are, the more likely we will have to make a decision that they will consider an offense. Of course, we must be very careful that we are being persecuted because of our righteous stand for Christ and not because of our own foolishness.

By trying to please people and live up to their expectations of us, we can easily fall into a false form of spirituality. We find ourselves praying, reading Scripture and worshiping, not from the heart, but from a desire to impress others. We become more interested in how we look to others than how we look to God. The more insecure we are the more susceptible we become to the opinions of others. Humility frees us from this form of pride to live to please the Lord.

Dear Lord, How easy it is to get my eyes off you and onto those around me. I am so easily swayed by what they think. Yet I have declared you, not others, to be the Lord of my life. I want everything I do to count for eternity and be pleasing in your sight. Teach me to be sensitive to how others feel, but not to be dominated by their opinions and expectations. I surrender any right I may have to look good in the eyes of other people. Please lead me and I will obey, even if that causes me to look foolish in the eyes of others.

Flattery

"A lying tongue hates those it hurts, and a flattering mouth works ruin" (Prov 26:28).

Compliments and flattery are not the same thing. When someone offers a compliment, his or her aim is to sincerely uplift the other person. The person who is a flatterer, however, has a different motive. Flattery is often used as bait. It is dangled before people to probe their loyalties and vulnerabilities. If the bait is taken, the flatterer has found a weakness which can be exploited. Flattery is designed to manipulate—it is an attempt to win another person's favor by saying nice things about them. It is comparing people, making one person feel superior to another.

Look at the way flattery is worded, and you will clearly see this: "You're so much more understanding than my husband." "You're better-looking than your sisters, aren't you?" "I can trust you. You're not like other Christians I've met. I can tell you really love me." On the surface these seem to be compliments, but there is a subtle appeal to a person's pride.

What can be done about flattery? If we are in the habit of

flattering others, then we must stop. Ask God for sincere compliments that can be offered in the place of flattery. When we are "victims" of flattery, we need to be honest with the person. Say to them: "I appreciate the way you are trying to encourage me, but I find it difficult when you mention other people's weaknesses. I would rather you didn't compare me to others in a way that puts them down. It makes me feel uncomfortable."

Dear Lord, When my heart is not pure before you I am capable of using words in an insincere attempt to manipulate people and situations. I want my heart to be pure before you. I want to be freed from flattery. Expose this sin, Lord, no matter what the cost is to me. No longer do I want to flatter people, and neither do I want to fall prey to flattery myself. Instead, I want to give and receive encouragement from the heart. Set a guard around my ears and mouth, convict me when I fall short. I do not wish to work ruin in my life or anyone else's. Lord, teach me your ways.

Self-Pity

"Be joyful always; pray continually; give thanks in all circumstances, for this is God's will for you in Christ Jesus" (1 Thess 5:16-18).

Self-pity is a direct result of failing to turn our problems over to the Lord, instead clinging to our hurts, frustrations and disappointments. Why do we have such difficulty in turning our burdens over to the Lord? Basically, because we think we can do a better job of dealing with them ourselves and because we enjoy the attention that comes when others feel sorry for us. If only we realized the love and peace of heart we are looking for is found by putting our problems in God's hands.

Do you feel overwhelmed with the pressures of your work or ministry, or with personal problems or tragedy? I felt that way when I first moved to Amsterdam. I was leading a team aboard two houseboats permanently anchored on a downtown canal. Many young people were coming off the streets for help and turning to the Lord. It was an exciting time, but it also put me under a great deal of pressure. I was responsible for fifty-five people, many of whom were young and inexperienced.

One day I lapsed into total self-pity. I thought, "Nobody understands me. Nobody cares about my needs, yet I always have to look out for their needs. I don't want this responsibility anymore." In that frame of mind I caught a ferry across the harbor and sat alone on the far bank. Tears streamed down my face as I poured my heart out to God. "I don't think I can stay in this ministry. I can't handle the pressure."

The Lord answered me, but not in the way I expected. He told me he wanted to expand me! He wanted me to do more, and if I allowed him free rein in my life he would increase my capacity for the job. Something broke inside me that day. It was my pride. I had been trying to carry things on my own and not asking the Lord for his help. I had failed to see that the burdens and responsibilities of leadership were ultimately his, not mine, and as a result I had fallen into self-pity.

When we are hurt, used, presumed upon, misunderstood, oppressed or sinned against, it is easy to lapse into self-pity. Self-pity will ultimately destroy us if we don't catch it and break the habit. It is also very easy to allow thought patterns of self-pity to be established when we are disappointed or depressed. Self-pity feeds our pride and excuses the selfish attention it thrives on. Self-pity is never satisfied; because it is selfish, it demands more and more.

Dear Lord, Your word says to rejoice in all circumstances. How often I am guilty of not doing this. I complain about my load, and compare myself to others who seem to have things easier. I feel sorry for myself, especially when I am hurt or disappointed. I recognize this as sin. Teach me to cooperate with you in what you are doing in my life, rather than rebelling. When I can see no good coming out of the things I am going through, help me to trust. I know you are committed to the highest good for my life. Teach me to think of others and not myself. Help me break this ever-deepening cycle of pity and self-centeredness.

Questions for Individuals or Groups

1. Why is pride like cancer (pp. 117)?
2. How can pride be a form of stealing from God (p. 118)?
3. What are some ways you've seen a demanding spirit in your life, of requiring that things be done your way (p. 120-21)?
4. How can we become more aware of our sometimes-unconscious attitudes of superiority toward those in other churches or ethnic groups or economic classes (pp. 121-22)?
5. Why is sarcasm or critical speech such an easy habit to fall into (pp. 123-25)?
6. How can you combat it?
7. Why is a lack of generosity a form of pride (pp. 127-28)?
8. On page 130 the author says, "The more mature we become in the Lord, the more we welcome the input and correction of others." Do you agree or disagree with this statement? Why or why not?
9. By trying to please people and live up to their expectations of what a good Christian is, we can sometimes fool ourselves into thinking that we are more

spiritual than others (pp. 132-33). How can you tell the difference between false piety and true devotion to God?

10. Those in ministry can be especially susceptible to self-pity (pp. 134-35). When has this been a struggle for you?

11. How can we get a healthy perspective on the work we do for God?

Eleven

Humility: Focusing on Christ

IF, while reading the preceding chapter, you have identified areas of pride in your life which seem overwhelming—don't despair. God does not reveal our sin to make us despondent and discouraged. Instead, he wants to help us overcome sin. By revealing our pride, God is showing us a wall between us and himself which, if left unchecked, will sever that relationship.

Pride is the one vice that no one on this planet is free of. It is something we all loath when we confront it in others, but do not imagine it is in ourselves. As C. S. Lewis has said, "There is no fault which we are more unconscious of in ourselves, and the more we have it in ourselves, the more we dislike it in others."

Perhaps our goal in seeking victory over pride should not be

simply freedom from pride, but to have the opposite of pride—
humility. Our focus should be Christlikeness, which is the essence of humility. Our concern then would not be focused on
getting rid of something, but on a more positive attitude of
yielding to the Lord Jesus so that he can make us like himself.
It is far better to say yes to Jesus than to say no to sin.

The Importance of Humility

It is said that Martin Luther was once asked to name the great-
est Christian virtue. He replied, "Humility." And the second?
"Humility" was again the response. And the third? "Humility."
It is the greatest of the virtues because it unlocks all other
virtues to us. Humility is the soil in which all other fruit of the
Spirit can grow.

The story is also told that one of the finest and wisest Christians in the sixteenth century, Philip Neri, was asked by the
pope to travel to a convent near Rome and meet a certain
novice who was reputed to be a saint. Neri rode on his mule
through the mud and the mire of country roads in the winter
to the convent. Arriving there, he asked that the novice be sent
to him. When she entered the room, he asked her to take off
his boots caked in mud from the long journey. She drew back
in anger and refused to do the menial task. She was affronted
at the very idea that she, with her reputation, should be asked
to do such a thing.

Neri said no more. He left the convent and went back to
Rome. "Don't wonder any longer," he said to the pope. "Here
is no saint, for here is no humility."

Consider the importance God's Word puts on humility:

Whoever humbles himself like this child is the greatest in the kingdom of heaven. (Mt 18:4)

For the LORD takes delight in his people; he crowns the humble with salvation. (Ps 149:4)

Toward the scorners he is scornful, but to the humble he shows favor. (Prov 3:34 RSV)

God opposes the proud but gives grace to the humble. (Jas 4:6).

What Humility Is Not

Many have a faulty view of humility. They associate it with a certain tremor in the voice when pious people pray or with the color of clothes one wears (black, of course!), especially on Sunday. Others fear that humility requires having their secret sins made known to one and all. Many criminals are caught and have their crimes exposed in the media, but they do not grow in humility. God has no desire to embarrass us through public ridicule.

Humility is also not a form of self-hatred. Some false expressions of spirituality suggest we punish ourselves until we drive out all sin within us. God created us, and his intention was that we be conformed to his image so that we become whole people deeply aware of our dependence on him and profoundly alive to his love and grace. Such confidence is the result of knowing that we have been forgiven by the Lord Jesus and transformed by his grace.

There is nothing worse than having to beg someone to do what they are qualified to do, only to find them feigning a false spirituality. Humility is not pretending we cannot do something that in reality we are trained or gifted to do. Nor is it a low estimate of our spiritual gifts and natural abilities.

Some people treat humility as a mystical experience, something that suddenly happens to us. But it is not mysteriously going to come over us of its own volition. Humility must be made the object of special desire and prayer. It is not something God does to us, but something we are to do before God—and others. Humility before God is nothing if it is not proven before others.

Peter instructed Christians many years ago to humble themselves (1 Pet 5:6). James, the brother of Jesus, also understood that humility must be chosen, using virtually the same words: "Humble yourselves before the Lord" (Jas 4:10).

Contrary to what might be expected, humility is not appreciated or desired by some people. It is seen as weakness in our culture. People are not expected to admit their mistakes or ask forgiveness. Humility is Christlikeness, and not all people want others around them who are like our Lord.

What Humility Is

What is humility? It is first of all dependence on God. It involves us, the creatures, acknowledging absolute and total dependence on God, the Creator. This is more than mere recognition that God has created us. Dependence that is the fruit of humility is an attitude that comes from our relationship with God. It requires our daily looking to God as a friend, as the one true source of forgiveness and mercy, and as the one who gives counsel and direction in every important decision of life.

Humility is a longing in the heart for a deep relationship with God. Even for people who do not know God, there is a deep awareness that something is missing. Once humble people discover that God loves them and offers forgiveness through Jesus Christ, they long to know more. In fact, they long to know God.

Christian service done for God may satisfy the soul for a period of time, but there comes a moment when the dry ground of the human spirit cries out for more than it has experienced before. Our tendency is to substitute form for reality, action for relationship and busyness for communion. Humility says that we must no longer substitute doing for being or religious fervor for spiritual reality. Humility drives us past religion—whether it be pageant, pilgrimage or penance. All of these can speak about God, but no religious form or symbol in the end can substitute for a personal encounter with the living God.

Finally, humility is release from hiding and pretending. Humility is a willingness to be known for who we really are. We live in a world that rewards superficiality and encourages covering up weaknesses, faults, wounds and secret sins.

By saying that we should be honest about past failures or present weaknesses, I am not suggesting that we must tell everyone everything about ourselves. There is a place for discretion. It does mean, however, that we come to terms with our fears and failures, and we share them with godly people who are close to us.

Honesty about our shortcomings should become a way of life. For example, if we fail to fulfill our responsibilities at work, we should not seek to cover them up, but admit that we were wrong and ask for forgiveness. And if we offend a family member, we should also humble ourselves and apologize for our insensitivity and impatience.

Straightforward admission of our needs, problems and shortcomings allows us to be free from the deceit of pride. We must be as open as we need to be to get help and freedom from our problems. We can receive the love, understanding and support we need in times of stress and difficulty by being honest.

Covering up our sins, even the "little ones," always catches up with us. Little compromises turn into big failures. People lose respect for us and find it hard to trust us when we cover up our mistakes and shortcomings. When people discover through another person that we have not been completely honest, they lose trust. We are then tempted to add manipulation to our pride and lying to our lack of humility. Ruthless honesty is the only way to break this pattern of deception.

Cultivating Humility

When I write about humility, I am not addressing a subject for the "holy." This is not a quality of life that is to be developed by an elite few. All Christians who take their commitment to Jesus Christ seriously recognize the great need to cultivate this virtue. Our integrity as believers hinges on our response to the command to humble ourselves.

Paul makes it clear in his writings that humility is to affect every area of our life. To the first-century believers, he said:

Be completely humble and gentle; be patient, bearing with one another in love. Make every effort to keep the unity of the Spirit. (Eph 4:2-3)

Do nothing out of selfish ambition or vain conceit, but in humility consider others better than yourselves. Each of you should not only look to your own interests, but also to the interests of others. (Phil 2:3-4)

Therefore, as God's chosen people, holy and dearly loved, clothe yourselves with compassion, kindness, humility, gen-

tleness and patience. Bear with each other and forgive whatever grievances you may have against one another. Forgive
as the Lord forgave you. (Col 3:12-14)

Each of the following sections explores how humility relates to
various areas of our daily lives. I suggest that after you read
them through, you go back through these meditations on a daily
basis, asking God to apply each one to your life in a practical
way. Begin each reading by asking the Holy Spirit to show you
your heart as God sees it, and how God wants to help you
humble yourself. As we humble ourselves in response to the
dealings of the Holy Spirit, God promises to give us more
grace.

Focusing on the Lord

The one who stands at the center of our lives has a lot to do
with humility. In comparing the worldly and the spiritual person in Romans 7—8, Paul focuses on the relative self-centeredness of each. Worldly people are preoccupied with self. They are
the center of their own universes. Indeed, the word *I* is used
twenty-five times in the passage that describes such a carnal
person. By contrast *I* is used only twice in the description of the
spiritual person. We can only wholeheartedly focus on one
thing at a time. Either we are focusing on ourselves or on the
Lord, living supremely for God or for ourselves.

By choosing to focus on the Lord we are freed from preoccupation with ourselves. Conversely, pride holds us a prisoner
to self-righteousness, self-pity, self-love, self-sufficiency, self-
congratulation and self-indulgence. Humility frees us from this
wretched state and allows us to enjoy God and others in a way
proud people cannot (Col 3:12-13).

Serving Others

It is one of the great paradoxes of Christianity that to be great in the kingdom means being the servant of all. Christ is our example. But Jesus "made himself nothing, taking the very nature of a servant" (Phil 2:7). The person who serves the most in the kingdom is the person who understands that Jesus became a servant for them. With this revelation their motivation in the Christian life is to serve as they have been served.

Nothing more clearly reveals the motives of the heart than how we react when asked to serve others. Do we consider some tasks below our dignity? Do we feel we're too mature in the Lord to mow the pastor's lawn or work in the nursery? Are we too busy to help with the lowliest jobs?

A large inner-city convent had a nun who always sang hymns while hanging out the laundry. There was an infectious quality of joy about her. A young novice, after several weeks at the convent, was intrigued by this older nun and asked why she was always so joyful.

The older nun replied, "The Lord called me to serve here many years ago, and I find it a privilege to hang out the laundry for others." The novice was impressed with this attitude, but was even more blessed when she heard the full story.

For many years this nun had been the Mother Superior of the convent until she grew too old to carry the load of responsibility. She had been offered a position with less responsibility in a smaller convent, but felt God had specifically called her to the convent she was in. The only other position at that time was for a laundry person. So she gladly took the position.

I was challenged when I heard this story. That nun had a calling from God to serve, and she was determined to fulfill the calling. Her heart to serve was clearly revealed to all when she chose a lowly position that would allow her to continue serving. She knew her true spirituality did not depend on any title she had been given in the past, but on her willingness to serve the Lord through serving others.

Learning from Others

Pride causes us to have a very narrow perspective on life. We believe we have all the right answers and so do not recognize the need to learn from others. Humility, by contrast, realizes there is something of value to be learned from everyone.

We need the broader perspective on life that humility can bring. It doesn't mean we're to be tossed to and fro like leaves in the wind, believing everything we're told. But it does mean we recognize our need for input from others. None of us possess the answers to all the situations of life, and so we need to learn from each other.

Could it be that God does not give a full revelation of truth to any single individual or group in order to keep us dependent on one another? We need the input of people from every part of the body of Christ. If we fail to acknowledge this need we will miss out on much of what God wants to reveal to us.

Encouraging Others

Giving encouragement is an easy and painless way to develop humility. It also changes our perspective on other people. To encourage others we have to search for their good points and lay aside all criticism and comparison, concentrating sincerely only on their strengths. Pride wants to hold us back from giving encouragement and instead focus on jealousy, mistrust and contempt. Encouraging others is a joyous experience for humble people, and if we're having difficulty giving it, we need to go to the Lord and ask him to show us why.

Trusting Others

God has entrusted to us the most precious gift of all—his love and trust. But are we worthy of that trust? Do we consistently live up to the level of trust God has placed in us? I know I haven't. I have failed the Lord many times. When I have repented, God has always given me another chance.

Do we extend that same trust to others? Or, do we say, "You've disappointed me. Never again!" If I am to be humble, I will give others the same love and trust God has given me. By withholding trust from a person who is truly sorry for the mistake they have made, we indulge our pride. We're saying to them, "You're not good enough. You cannot meet my standard and you never will."

Trusting anyone in this sinful, fallen world is a risky business. Yet God seems to think it is a risk worth taking! He does not trust us because we are perfect, but because of his mercy toward us. His trust is based on grace and not on our performance. We must make sure grace is the basis of the trust we put in others.

Laying Down Our Rights

Our society is based on personal rights. These rights come in a variety of forms: the right to a home, a private bedroom, a hot bath, three meals a day and the right to defend ourselves when attacked or when our reputation is endangered. We also feel we have a right to be consulted when decisions are made that have an impact on our lives. The prevailing mentality of our society with regard to rights seems to be: If I don't look out for my rights, I won't get anywhere in life.

Christians, however, march to the beat of a different drum. Jesus is our example when it comes to rights. He was accused, maligned and betrayed, yet not once did he fight for his rights. He forgave his accusers, blessed those who persecuted him and willingly laid down his life.

Seeking Justice

When we first moved into the inner city, we talked with our children about our ministry plans. We had some wonderful discussions with our two little ones, Matthew and Misha. One day Misha said that she thought we should move into the red light district because it would make Jesus happy.

"Why?" we asked, rather astonished.

"Well, it says in that song we sing that he has shown us what is good, that we should do justly, love mercy and walk humbly with our God!"

Out of the mouths of babes! We sang Micah 6:8 in our community worship times, and at six years of age Misha had listened and understood the meaning of the words. The verse says, "He has showed you, O man, what is good. And what does the LORD require of you? To do justly and to love mercy and to walk humbly with your God."

People are not just sinners, they are sinned against, and we are called to defend the rights of the poor (Prov 31:8-9). When revival comes to a nation, as it did in the time of Charles Finney, people will be confronted with their sins against the oppressed. The gospel must be applied to social mores and standards if we are to take it seriously. For Finney that meant confronting slavery and speaking for the emancipation of women.

We may be scorned, mocked, misunderstood and ridiculed for doing so, but if we as Christians stand by silently in the face of racism, poverty, injustice, exploitation of the earth's resources and gross inequality, then we have given in to the opinions of others. Our pride has gotten in the way of the gospel. We must lay aside public opinion and speak for those who have no voice. It is the humble thing to do.

Admitting Our Needs and Weaknesses

Ironically, the key to victory in the Christian life is found in learning how to handle failure! Christ's power is made perfect in weakness. If we say we're not weak, we have no need of his power in our lives. Conversely, when we acknowledge our limitations and weaknesses we are freed to ask the Lord and others for their help.

"If we claim to be without sin, we deceive ourselves and the truth is not in us" (1 Jn 1:8). None of us is perfect, and we should not act as if we are. A proud man covers his weaknesses while the humble man admits them. Humility frees us from the fear of failure and allows us to embrace the love and affirmation of others—which we all need. Admitting our weaknesses, especially feelings of inferiority, is one of the surest ways to overcome our insecurities.

In some instances an inferiority complex is only pride. You can never have real humility while you are preoccupied with yourself. God wants to help us break out of our self-centeredness and self-consciousness and be free to think of others and their needs. All it takes is humility—confessing our fears to those around us.

Seeing Ourselves As Others See Us

It would be interesting if we were able to step outside our bodies and see ourselves as others see us. While we can never be that objective, by listening to others and receiving with genuine thanks any criticism they may have of us, we can obtain, in small part, an objective view of our lives. Ask God and your friends to help you evaluate your strengths and weaknesses. Choose to be known for who you are. Hide nothing. Regularly confess your weaknesses, temptations and sins, asking God for his forgiveness. Make it a daily commitment, and as you follow through on it, you will become more and more like the Lord Jesus.

Always remember, humility is the result of godly living. Through depending on God, hungering to know him and acknowledging any areas of sin or weakness we have, humility will grow in our lives.

Questions for Individuals or Groups

1. What are common stereotypes of humility (pp. 141-42)?

2. How would you define *humility*?

3. The author first suggests that humility is dependence on God (p. 142). Give some examples of how this kind of dependence can express humility.

4. Next, McClung says, "Humility is a longing in the heart for a deep relationship with God" (p. 142). Explain how this fits into the nature of humility.

5. Third, the author says, "Humility is a willingness to be known for who we really are" (p. 143). Why isn't it necessary to tell everyone everything to be able to exemplify this characteristic of humility?

6. What are some practical ways we can focus on the Lord as a step toward humility (p. 144-51)?

7. Think of the Christians in your small group or a few at your church. What could you say to each one about their strengths that would be encouraging? (Make plans to write, call or tell those people in person.)

8. What are some of the ways our society influences us to stand up for our rights (pp. 148-49)?

9. McClung writes, "The gospel must be applied to social mores and standards if we are to take it seriously" (p. 149). Do you agree or disagree? Explain.

10. What are ways you could seek justice in your community?

11. Consider who you might ask to give you an objective evaluation of your strengths and weaknesses (p. 150). Ask God to help you receive these comments with openness and humility.

Twelve

Wholehearted Friendship

JOE has a great relationship with his five-year-old son, Nick. It's the sort of relationship that makes me smile when I see them together with their heads bent over an anthill they've come upon, or running and laughing while flying a homemade kite in a field.

I once commented to Joe that I admired the way he took so much time out from his already-crowded schedule to spend time with his son. His response was interesting. He told me he wanted Nick to grow up and embrace his ideals—to love serving the Lord and care for the world around him. Joe felt that for Nick to enter into his world, he first had to enter into his son's world, and so he worked at becoming his son's best friend. Joe built bridges into Nick's life through playing games with him, talking, listening and caring.

Joe's desire to reach out to his son is very much like God's desire to be our friend. Jesus entered our world to show us the Father. He came as a friend to those who needed him. In John's Gospel Jesus tells us, "As the Father has sent me, I am sending you" (Jn 20:21). Jesus wants us to reach out to others as he reaches out to us. This is one of the signs of wholehearted commitment.

Will I Witness Today?

The primary reason the Father sent the Lord Jesus was to reconcile people to himself. That is why Jesus sends us as well. As we wholeheartedly seek to obey our Lord, we should look to his example in fulfilling the Father's mission for our lives. Jesus' death on the cross is our message, and the way he came to people is our model.

If we think that witnessing is merely preaching or handing out tracts on the streets on a Friday night, we miss the wider implication of our lives as witnesses. Witnessing cannot be turned off and on like a machine—it is not just an act of the will. It is not just something we do; it is who we are.

Some years ago in the northwestern United States, a prominent minister was visiting outlying parishes under his pastoral care. In one town he stayed at the local hotel for several days, and as he was checking out the desk clerk, assuming him to be a traveling salesman, asked what he was selling. "What do you think I sell?" the minister replied.

The clerk was quick to guess. "Oh, I bet you're a whisky salesman." The minister did not reply and walked away saddened, wondering what it was in his behavior that had led the clerk to make such a conclusion. Likewise, people constantly draw conclusions about us based solely on how they see us live and act.

Integrity in witnessing occurs when our words line up with the way we live our lives. Paul, writing to the church at Corinth, says, "For the kingdom of God is not a matter of talk but of power" (1 Cor 4:20). Powerful evangelism is evangelism that has integrity, that flows from a life committed to being a faithful witness.

Many of us have heard or read the testimonies of people who said the way a Christian reacted to a situation made them rethink their opinion of Christianity. They were so impressed by the quality of life they saw that they began searching for it. What do people think of us when we are under stress? Even the "little things" in our lives can have a significant impact on others.

In Amsterdam, as in all big cities, we spend a lot of time waiting in lines in the shops and department stores we frequent. Enetha, one of my coworkers, tries to always ask God for extra patience and friendliness when she has to wait. Recently she found herself the last in line to be served at a gift shop. Some of those ahead of her were becoming irritable and restless, so when Enetha's turn came, she purposely reacted in a different manner from those ahead of her.

She commented on how nice the salesperson was and asked her name. She found out it was Marie and asked her if it was a family name. Marie explained how her parents had known a wonderful Christian woman named *Marie,* and she had been named after her. Marie went on to tell Enetha she only attended church twice a year and had been wondering lately if that was "all there was to being a Christian"! They agreed to meet later and continue the conversation. At their next meeting Marie confided that she had no idea why she mentioned about going to church, but had been so impressed by the way Enetha acted toward her that she just found herself pouring out her heart.

Jesus pointed out to the Pharisees that "out of the overflow of the heart the mouth speaks" (Mt 12:34). If our hearts are not filled with love for God, it will soon show in our words. We cannot lead a person any closer to Jesus than we are ourselves. We cannot pass on to another person a spiritual truth unless it is first a firm reality in our lives. Thus, we must understand the nature of Christ's ministry on earth in order to understand how we should go about ministering to others.

What Was Christ Like?

First, Jesus gave up his rights in order to come to us. He left his home, gave up fellowship with his Father, and laid aside every divine right he had. We live in a "rights"-oriented world. Everyone is conscious of and demands what is rightfully his or hers. People who give up their rights, particularly in order to build friendships and solve conflicts with others, have the power of unselfish love on their side. This way of living is attractive because of its unselfishness.

Second, Jesus was a servant. " 'Do you understand what I have done for you?' he asked them. 'You call me "Teacher" and "Lord," and rightly so, for that is what I am. Now that I, your Lord and Teacher, have washed your feet, you also should wash one another's feet' " (Jn 13:12-14).

In the Western world we are so familiar with the gospel that we lose sight of the astounding paradoxes in it. The Son of God came into our world to be a servant! In today's world where authority denotes rank, it's hard to imagine the head of a major corporation assigning his capable son to scrub the office floors for thirty-three years. If there's one person in the universe who deserves to be served it is Jesus, the Son of the Living God, yet he came not to be served, but to serve.

Third, Jesus came as a friend. He was available to people in all manner of situations. He encouraged people. He listened to them. He was honest, forgiving and accepting. He had principles, so was respected. In short, he was a genuine friend. He was the kind of person whom people felt could understand their problems.

Finally, Jesus was obedient. "My food is to do the will of him who sent me and to finish his work" (Jn 4:34). Jesus' obedience stood strong, even when tested to its limits in the Garden of Gethsemane as he anguished over his impending death on the cross. This commitment to truth gave Jesus genuine spiritual authority. He came to do the work of his Father (Jn 12:49). Because of his love for truth, people were attracted to him.

So, Jesus came to earth as a servant. He had authority, gave up his rights and was obedient to his Father, even when that meant an excruciating death. In the same way he sends us to others. It is not enough to just have zeal and enthusiasm. If we are to be effective in evangelism, we must go about it in the same manner as Jesus did.

The Gospels record Jesus ministering in a variety of situations. He stood on the side of a mountain and taught the multitudes about the kingdom of God. He spoke with a Samaritan woman as she drew water from a well. He fed five thousand people and ate privately at the home of Zaccheus, the tax collector. Whether it was a few people or many, he was always comfortable and able to minister with power and effectiveness. He took the time to identify with his audience. He listened to them. And when he found out their needs, he ministered to them. Let's consider these three principles of evangelism so we can effectively follow his model. To be effective evangelists we must follow his pattern.

Identifying

Occasionally people say to me, "I could never do what you are doing—I could never live in the inner city, talk to a drug addict, a prostitute or an alcoholic." I respond by telling people that identification with non-Christians does not depend on what we have been through in the past, but on what the Holy Spirit does in our hearts now. I am the guy who tried to smoke half of a cigarette when I was a boy, and it made me sick!

The computer programmer who has rejected Christ is as much a sinner as a prostitute, thief or murderer. It does not matter whether a person is drowning five feet from the side of a swimming pool or five miles out to sea; the fact is that person is drowning and is in need of rescue.

Jewish culture in Jesus' day was very structured: lepers were outcasts; women were subservient; doctrinal differences created permanent rifts. The Samaritans, for example, had different views on where God should be worshiped, and they had inter-married with the Assyrians. This completely separated them from the mainstream of Jewish life and culture.

Against this background, Jesus came and touched the lepers, spoke to and respected women, walked through Samaria and talked to its inhabitants and taught all who would listen. Jesus was without sin, yet he did not condemn the people he ministered to. Instead he showed them the utmost respect. He put himself in their place, felt what they felt, laughed when they laughed, and cried when they cried. In so doing, he identified with them and their needs.

Having been forgiven by God, we have all the more reason to identify with those we are reaching out to. Identification in evangelism means that, without compromise, we enter into the life and feelings of those to whom we are witnessing. When we respond to people out of genuine love and respect, the walls they have built around their lives begin to crumble.

Listening

All too often in our eagerness to talk to people about the gospel, we fail to take the time to listen to their concerns. We start conversations in which we don't really want to hear the other person's point of view. We are just waiting for a lull in the conversation so we can pounce in with our prepackaged gospel presentation.

We need to listen intelligently to other people to ask questions and find out what their views are. As we draw a person's thoughts out, we can rephrase what they have said to be sure we understand them. When a person senses we are interested in what they are saying, they are likely to open up further. And we have a lot to learn from others!

Body language is also important to being a good listener. If our mouths are saying one thing and our bodies another, the person we are speaking to will be confused. Watch tendencies to fidget, to look elsewhere and do other distracting things which unconsciously convey a lack of interest in what the person is saying.

It is also good to remember the names of people you talk to. This is not always easy, but asking their names and then using it several times in the first few minutes of conversation is one way to help lodge it in your mind. If you think you will see them again, write down their names and memorize them. Remember to pray for them as well.

All of this adds up to showing respect for the person we are witnessing to. When people talk to us, they tell us things that matter to them, and if, in our opinion, their views are strange, illogical, weird or unreasonable, we must still show respect. People have a right to their views, and we should be honored that they took the time to share them with us.

Responding in Love and Wisdom

Though a person's separation from God is his or her most obvious need to us as Christians, it is not necessarily that which must be addressed first. Other needs, such as friendship and acceptance, a place to stay, food to eat, dignity and self-esteem, are often the felt needs of the person you want to befriend. Taking care of those needs will open a door of friendship through which we can minister to their needs to know Christ as Savior.

There are three basic inherited human needs that are common to us all. These needs must be recognized and respected in all human relationships. Evangelism that ignores these needs can end up being very impersonal in nature.

First, all people have a need to belong and to be wanted. God created us as social beings. We were created for friendship and relationship. No program of evangelism can meet this need. There is simply no replacement for genuine friendship and acceptance.

Then there is the need for significance and importance. We all want and appreciate respect and dignity. We are created in God's image; therefore, we have value. Our choices have meaning, even when they are the wrong choices. When we approach people, it should be with the utmost respect for their opinions, ideas and choices. We give affirmation to others and thus help affirm their worth and value before God when we treat them in this manner.

The third human need is for security and safety. When this need is not met, the result is fear—one of the most powerful human emotions. By being sensitive to people, by loving them and being kind, we create room for security in the relationship. Love drives away fear, but a lack of love creates insecurity and uncertainty, which is never conducive to evangelism.

Larry and Jan moved into a new apartment building about a year and a half ago. Soon they were busy introducing themselves to their new neighbors. Over time their friendly, outgoing attitude and their willingness to listen to their neighbors had an effect on the residents of the apartment building.

About nine months later, a couple from a neighboring apartment came to visit unexpectedly. With tears in their eyes they explained how the Jehovah's Witnesses had come to their door wanting them to change their religion. They recognized that Larry and Jan were different from the Jehovah's Witnesses. They had cared for them, respected them, listened and understood what they were feeling. As a result, this couple wanted to know more about Larry's and Jan's faith in God. The four of them now have a regular Bible study together.

A Consistent Lifestyle
Jan and Larry had learned the secret of reaching people through

modeling their lives after Christ. God could have written the instructions for salvation in the sky. Instead, he chose the most intimate and personal of ways—he sent his Son. Jesus lived his life openly and in full view of others. He invited the disciples to learn both from what he said and from how he lived his life. We must do the same if we are to be credible witnesses. Words lack the power to bring conviction and change if they are not reflected in the life of the person speaking.

Several years ago some workers from Youth With A Mission went to establish a ministry among Vietnamese refugees who were being held in a camp in Hong Kong. When they first asked for permission to enter the camp it was denied, but they persisted and were eventually allowed to enter. The camp supervisor, however, suspecting them to be just another group of "do-gooders" who would not last, forbade them to do anything "evangelistic." Instead, they were assigned to work at restoring a blocked and overflowing toilet system. For days the team labored knee-deep in squalid waste. They scrubbed, cleaned and mended broken and blocked pipes until the toilet system was once again fully operational.

When they reported to the supervisor for their next task, he confided that he'd never expected them to complete the first one. He was so impressed with their attitude and willingness to work that he opened the camp to them to run evangelistic programs. The team soon found that the Vietnamese people, who had watched closely as they restored the broken toilet system, had been touched by what they saw. They were ready and eager to listen to the gospel message that the team had to share with them.

Everything we choose to do, or not to do—our attitudes, the

way we treat others, our words—all have an impact on some-one. We cannot go through a day or week without our life influencing somebody. The question is not *whether* we will witness, but *how*.

Questions for Individuals or Groups

1. Why is witnessing more than preaching or handing out tracts (pp. 154-56)?

2. Why is merely allowing people to watch the way we live life not an adequate witness either?

3. How did Jesus minister while on earth (pp. 156-58)?

4. What are some practical ways in witnessing that you could imitate the way Jesus gave up his rights, became a servant, became a friend or was obedient to the Father?

5. What does it mean to identify with others the way Jesus did (pp. 158-59)?

6. Think of a non-Christian you know. How could you identify with that person?

7. What problem can it create when we don't find out what people think or adequately listen to them before we try to present the gospel (pp. 158-59)?

8. What are some simple ways we can show people we want to listen and know about them?

9. What are the three basic human needs the author says we all have (pp. 159-60)?

10. How do you feel one or more of these needs in your own life?

11. How could you make yourself available to meet these kinds of needs in the lives of those around you?

Thirteen

Finding a Common Ground

RECENTLY I flew to South Africa. A young lady sat across the aisle from me, and we began a conversation. We started by talking about the weather, how calm the flight was and other things of that nature. As the conversation developed, she told me she worked with KLM Airlines and had been in Amsterdam for a training program. I asked about her work and how she enjoyed it, all the while praying the Lord would lead in our conversation.

Eventually she asked me what I did. Calmly I responded, "I work with prostitutes in Amsterdam." She gave me a surprised look, and I went on to tell her that we—myself, my wife and our two young children—live in the red light district of the city. I described to her, in fairly sociological terms at first, what we

were doing. As we continued, I began to weave the gospel more
and more into the conversation.

"The reason we're involved is because those women have
value, regardless of what they've done. I believe every person
has great value and worth to God."

She told me she was a Catholic and prayed to Mary. It
seemed her way of saying, "You believe your way and I will
believe mine." I noticed she watched me very intently to see
what my reaction was.

After the lapse of some time, she looked over and asked me
what I thought about praying to Mary.

I thought for a moment and felt the Spirit give me direction.
"I have a lot of Catholic friends. Some of them pray to Mary
because they don't feel they're worthy enough to pray to Jesus."

I became aware of the Holy Spirit's presence in my conversation at that moment. I explained how, during most of my
growing up years, I'd lived under a list of rules and had not
experienced a relationship with Jesus based on his love for me.
One day, as my college professor taught on Galatians, it suddenly hit me that God loves me. I could come to him and ask
his forgiveness based on his love for me. "That is the most
wonderful thing that ever happened to me," I told her.

Big tears rolled down her cheeks. "I've never heard anything
like that before. It's so beautiful."

At that moment the Holy Spirit was giving her an understanding of God's love for her. My goal was not to force something on her that she did not want but, in the context of mutual
respect for each other in spite of serious disagreements over our
beliefs, to share my understanding of the gospel. I had the sat-
isfaction of knowing she left the plane with a clear and deep

understanding of God's love for her.

Arousing Interest

We may not always have the luxury of time. We must understand the balance between the need to earn the right to speak about Christ and the Holy Spirit leading us to speak in a situation. On an airplane, for example, there is only limited time to speak with others. In such a situation we must follow the Spirit's leading. Perhaps he wants us to jump right into the conversation and ask about their interests in spiritual matters. If their response is negative, that's okay; don't force the issue. It is our responsibility to obey God—not to force a conversation.

Sometimes we may not want to open a religious conversation at all, but instead just talk to the person about his or her interests in life. Regardless of how we are led, we must be sensitive to the individual. If the person is interested, great. If not, we can pray for them.

As Christians, we often have a narrow field of interests which may leave us at a disadvantage. Not only does it confirm to the non-Christian's mind that Christians are boring and rather ignorant of the world around them, but it also provides us with little common ground. It is important for Christians to keep abreast of what is happening in the world. We should read as widely as possible. By broadening our horizons we provide ourselves with information that will help us to more easily enter into conversation.

I like to think witnessing is a little like fishing. You bait the hook and throw it into the water. If there's a nibble, you draw it in a little. Then you wait, draw the line in a little again, and wait for the fish to renew its interest. When you feel the fish has a firm hold of the bait and hook, you begin reeling it in.

In witnessing we follow the same procedure. Most Christians take the rod and beat "the fish" over the head, and then they wonder why they don't jump in the boat! We shouldn't give a twenty-point sermon on justification by faith and then make a quick exit when talking about God's love. Instead, we should whet a person's curiosity by sharing things that are precious to us in the hope that they will want to know more.

Jesus was a master of this. He told parables that aroused people's interest. They would think about what he had said and ask him for more clarification. From there he would go on and share the deeper truths he wanted to communicate. John chronicled Jesus' conversation with a Samaritan woman drawing water from a well. He used "living water" as a way of getting her attention. It caught the woman's curiosity and by the end of their conversation her life was touched and changed forever (Jn 4:4-42).

Evangelism is not just talking. Talking plays an important part in evangelism but, ultimately, it is the motive behind what we say and the attitude in which we speak, rather than the actual words we use, that makes the greatest impact. Genuineness and honesty, not eloquence, will win the hearts of men and women. People want to see that we really care for and understand them. Then they will open up to the message we have to share with them. It may take time, but it is time well spent. In the end, they don't care how much we know until they know how much we care.

Several years ago Janet, a worker with Youth With A Mission, was witnessing on Waikiki Beach in Hawaii. She struck up a conversation with a middle-aged man. When it became apparent to him that she was a Christian, he pulled a Bible from his shirt pocket. Janet was somewhat taken aback when he began flipping from one underlined passage to another which "proved" God was a vengeful and hateful God. Every time she said something, he would find another Scripture to confirm his distorted view of God until it became impossible to continue the conversation. This man had been hurt by the attitudes of Christians who had witnessed to him in the past. So, he had taken the trouble to study the Bible and carry it with him so he could ward off anyone else who tried to talk to him about the Lord.

Humility Not Humiliation

There are those Christians determined to bully others into agreeing with them regardless of the cost to human relationships. They do not understand that we are called to be witnesses, not warriors, in the cause of evangelism. We are not out to conquer by sheer force of will and words those we witness to.

Most of us have had a person from a cult come to our door and attempt to convince us they're right and we're wrong. It is an experience few of us enjoy! They may be sincere, yes, but they treat us more like objects than people. Their main aim seems to be getting through their pre-learned presentation.

While we may also feel uncomfortable and frustrated by this sort of approach ourselves, we often use it on non-Christians. I am not saying we shouldn't go door-to-door. We should! We should also go out on the streets, to the park, to shopping malls and to any other place where we can break into people's complacent lifestyles. The key, however, is to love people, not ma-

nipulate them. Let them sense our love and concern while chal-
lenging their minds. We should aim to present the gospel in
creative ways that will cause them to think. But in the end we
must respect their right and ability to make their own choice
about what we share.

I believe it is important to find common ground with the
person we're witnessing to. It is much easier to work from some
commonly held interest or belief than it is to attack a person's
beliefs, which only serves to put them on the defensive. Don't
ask people outright if they are Christians. If they answer yes,
but seem to have little grasp of what being a Christian really is,
we end up trying to catch inconsistencies in their beliefs so we
can show them they are not really a believer after all. That is
a negative way to witness.

Paul was the master at finding common ground. When addressing the philosophers at the Aeropagus, he did not say:
"Listen you misguided philosophers. Your God is dead. You're
wasting your time praying to idols. I have the right religion, so
be quiet and I will tell you about the true, loving and gracious
God."

Instead, he started out on common ground: "Men of Athens!
I see that in every way you are very religious. For as I walked
around and looked carefully at your objects of worship, I even
found an altar with this inscription: TO AN UNKNOWN GOD.
Now what you worship as something unknown I am going to
proclaim to you" (Acts 17:22-23).

Paul, after finding a point they agreed upon, goes on to give
a very clear summary of the gospel adapted to their understanding. "When they heard about the resurrection of the dead, some
of them sneered, but others said, 'We want to hear you again

on this subject. . . .' A few men became followers of Paul and believed" (Acts 17:32-34). It is questionable whether any of them would have believed had Paul started in by aggressively sharing the gospel and showing little regard for those in his audience.

The writer of Hebrews uses the same method. He anchors the Christian message to Jewish religion because it is the background of those he is writing to. His aim is to show them the truth by respecting their beliefs, and not to alienate them by attacking.

The most important point of all is to be a servant. As I've made clear in the last two chapters, it is essential that we take the route of humility. We should avoid putting ourselves above those we are trying to reach. We can freely admit our sins and weaknesses instead of dominating people by the sheer power of our personalities or the cleverness of our words. A humble attitude has more impact in evangelism than anything else we can do.

Planting, Not Forcing Growth

God does not sanction or require that we bring conviction of sin to those people we talk to about salvation. If we try to do this we have stepped over the line and taken upon us the job of the Holy Spirit. "When he [the Holy Spirit] comes, he will convict the world of guilt in regard to sin and righteousness and judgment" (Jn 16:8).

At times I have tried to be the Holy Spirit to others and have been totally frustrated. I have learned that in his own time and way, the Holy Spirit will do the convicting, regardless of how hard I, in my own strength, try to make it happen. We must always remember that in evangelism it is our job to sow the seed of the gospel in a person's heart. It is the job of the Holy Spirit to cause that seed to take root and bring forth a harvest of conviction, repentance and new life.

Choice Not Manipulation

It is easy to manipulate people, and we live in a world that subtly does it every day. Advertising bombards us from all sides trying to create false needs that will cause us to rush out and buy the products advertised. In such a world of manipulation we must be very careful not to employ the same means in evangelism.

Jesus did not manipulate people. He did not try to back them into corners where they could do nothing but what he wanted them to do. He always presented the truth in love and allowed people the latitude to act upon it as they saw fit. Many responded to his message, others chose not to. We must be careful to follow this example in our evangelism. Always remember that just as easily as you can manipulate a person into accepting the gospel and giving their life to Jesus, someone else can manipulate them out of it. People must choose for themselves based on the truth and love—that is the only way evangelism will be effective and long-lasting.

People Not Targets

I can remember, as a teen-ager, traveling back from outreach ministries. The teams would reunite and our conversation would run along these lines:

"How many did you get today?"

"Oh, I got eight."

"That's good, but I got thirteen. Five more than you!"

"Well, it was a slow day for me. I had trouble warming up, and wasted a lot of time talking to someone who was not really open."

As much as I hate to admit it, we were talking about leading people to Christ. Each "conversion" represented another notch on our Bible covers! We had entirely missed the point that people are not just objects to be won. We centered our attention on techniques that would get the highest number of affirmative responses instead of ministering to a person's needs.

The term *soul winning* is in popular use in Christianity today. In many ways it is a positive term which expresses our commitment as believers to make Christ known, but it can also be a negative term. It may give the impression that our goal is to win a person's soul, which can make us technique-oriented—we become dependent on diagrams and recited lines. If our ministry targets say yes at the appropriate points, they're "saved." If they say no the game is over, and it's time to go on to another person. People are not merely souls to be won. They are people to be loved and respected. To treat people only as "lost souls" is to reduce them to the level of an object, thus denigrating their value as someone created in God's image.

A Better Way

Jesus and his disciples presented the gospel in a variety of ways. The same approach is never recorded twice in the New Testament. Sometimes Jesus talked in parables. Other times he asked direct questions. He sent his disciples out two by two, but instead of giving them a pat formula to recite, he told them to be witnesses to what they had seen. If this approach was sufficient for the disciples, it should also be enough for us.

Our witnessing must be to the truth. The person we are witnessing to is not the focus, we are not trying to "get them." Instead, the focus is Jesus. We are witnessing to all he has done for us. All he requires of us is that we faithfully witness to the truth of what we understand and have experienced. It then becomes the job of the Holy Spirit to take our witness and use it to draw the person to Jesus. It is his job and we cannot do it for him.

It can be advantageous to learn how to effectively share our faith. It can be helpful to gather our thoughts into a systematic framework as we witness to the truth of what we know and have experienced. However, we must be careful not to use questions or approaches to witnessing in an assembly-line fashion on every person we meet. No one wants to feel they are the twenty-third person to have "Plan 5-B" tried on them.

Techniques are nothing more than tools which are sometimes appropriate to draw people into conversation and should be used sparingly and wisely. We, not our technique, are witnesses to the truth. No matter how elaborate and well crafted our technique is, our life, as a living reflection of Jesus, is what will touch the hearts of men and women.

If we're asked a question and don't know the answer, what should we do? We should be honest with the person and tell them we don't know the answer! Honesty is necessary and has a powerful effect when it comes from the heart. We are not trying to dazzle people with our knowledge; we are trying to communicate Jesus' love to them.

If a person asks honest questions, a lack of answers can be a barrier to the person making a commitment to Christ. If this is the case, then it needs to be answered. Write down the questions people ask, and go home and research the answer. Ask someone who knows more about it for their input.

Become familiar with good Christian literature which covers the most commonly asked questions (see the further reading section), and give that person an appropriate book. Plan to meet at a later date to discuss it. You may lose some books giving them out this way, but it is worth it for the joy of bringing a non-Christian into a relationship with Christ.

Patience
In an instant world it's easy to look for instant success. However, there are no shortcuts in friendship evangelism. No matter how good our tracts may be or how thorough our witnessing program is, there are no substitutes for taking time to develop relationships with the people we are seeking to lead to the Lord. There may be times when we spend weeks, months and even years just praying for a person's salvation before we ever have the opportunity to witness to them.

Over the past ten years, Sally and I have had our hair cut at a small salon located in one of Amsterdam's tourist hotels. The owner is gay, and some of the customers are prostitutes. However, we feel God wants us to go there and be real friends with the people who work there.

Marijke, our hairstylist, was very defensive when we tried to talk to her about the Lord and would refuse to talk at length about anything. I really wanted to talk with her and was discouraged by her response. At times I would pray all the way to the salon and while my hair was being cut and still nothing happened. However, when I was tempted to give up I always heard the Lord saying, "Be patient. I'm going to touch her heart."

Several months ago, a turning point came in an unusual way. A man came to the salon claiming to be a Christian. He asked one of the girls out and afterward tried to seduce her. Everyone at the salon was indignant about the incident. What had upset them most was that the man had said he was a Christian. The next time Sally went to the salon Marijke told her the story and commented, "That man was not a Christian like Floyd. I trust Floyd. He would never do a thing like that."

Not long afterward I went to have my hair cut. I said to Marijke: "Thank you for what you said to Sally. I'm glad you trust me. Sally and I both love you and are very committed to you." There was a breakthrough that day in our friendship. We are able to be open and honest with each other in a new way, and many times when I go to the salon, she wants to talk about Christian things. She is not a Christian yet, but she is softening each time we talk.

It took ten years of patience and perseverance with Marijke before the seeds of the gospel began to take root in her heart. At times it was frustrating and seemed pointless, but now those years of perseverance, of walking across town to the salon while I prayed fervently, are reaping results. Friendship evangelism is not for the impatient or intolerant.

Successful Evangelism
There is tremendous pressure to be someone of importance in our society, and in many respects, social status depends upon success. It is not surprising, then, that the same criteria is often used to evaluate evangelism.

Successful evangelism, however, is not based on the number of converts we've made, the variety of witnessing techniques we know, the length of time we can stand on a street corner handing out tracts, or what evangelism seminars we have attended. Some of these things may aid our evangelism, but they do not make us effective evangelists.

Successful evangelism is firmly rooted in our willingness to get personally involved in the lives of non-Christians with a view to being a faithful witness to Christ. If that life is shallow and ineffectual, then our evangelism will be the same. To be effective evangelists, we must first spend time developing our relationship with the Lord. That is not to infer we shouldn't share our faith until we are mature Christians—we should. What it means is that our emphasis must be on the quality of our Christian lives and not the words or techniques we use.

Jesus demonstrated this. It was his life, and not his words, which drew people. Indeed, there are instances recorded where the crowds had little idea of what he was talking about! Yet, there was a quality in his life that attracted and challenged all who came into contact with him.

In the final analysis it is God, not humans, who measures effectiveness in evangelism, and his standard has different reference points than ours. He is not going to judge us on the number of converts we have made in the course of our lives. He is more interested in how we have lived our lives before others and the impact that it has had on those around us. Yes, we must share the gospel—Jesus has commanded us to do so—but we must never forget we are dealing with people and not just statistics. We must respect people, honor them, win their confidence, and, in doing so, earn the right to speak with them about the Lord. When we make this our priority, the words we speak will deeply touch a person's life.

Getting Started

Perhaps you are wanting to know where to begin in sharing your faith. If you are looking for some specific steps and helps, let me suggest the following principles:

1. *Pray regularly for three or four friends who are not Christians.* Ask God for ways to serve your friends. Ask him how you can get more involved in their lives. Perhaps it will mean having them to your home or helping them at work. Perhaps a gift or a book would be meaningful.

2. *Establish social relationships with the people you are praying for.* Build friendships with them through activities they enjoy. Develop mutual interests. If you do not have such friends, it's time to start developing them.

3. *Respond to the felt needs of your friends.* What do they feel they need? Answers to questions? A job? Food to eat? Love and acceptance? Help with family problems? A sense of importance? Respond by getting involved.

4. *Get to know their objections to Christianity and give them thoughtful answers.* As we respond to people's questions, we can do so with the knowledge that as Christians, we have much to learn from them as well. We should cultivate an attitude of open inquiry and honest searching for truth. God has deposited the knowledge of himself in all religions and cultures, and although he has uniquely revealed himself through the Lord Jesus, there is much for us to learn from all faiths, cultures and political perspectives.

5. *Invite your friends to activities and events with other Chris-*

tians. We should be sensitive to what types of events they would be most comfortable attending. Hopefully, they can taste Christian fellowship and see the love of Christ as it is expressed between brothers and sisters in the Lord.

6. *If they show interest in spiritual things, offer to study the Bible with your friends, or invite them to a small group Bible study.* Exactly how and when a person may come to the Lord through our sharing the gospel we may never know. Witnessing is a process, and it is difficult to tell exactly what part each of us plays in drawing a person to Christ. Some of us may be working in fields that are "ready for harvest;" others of us are planting seeds amid the rocky ground. What is important is that each of us functions under the direction of the Lord of the harvest. We must concentrate on pleasing him. Jesus said, "But I, when I am lifted up from the earth, will draw all men to myself" (Jn 12:32). Let us always lift up Jesus as the one worthy of allegiance.

Questions for Individuals or Groups

1. When have you been uncomfortable when someone tried to force their views (whether religious or political or ethical) on you? Describe the situation.

2. What would have been a better way for that person to approach you that would have made you more receptive to their ideas?

3. Why is it often difficult to get non-Christians interested in the gospel?

4. What are bridges of common interest that we can use to help make Christian truth of interest to non-Christians?

5. Think of a recent item of prominence in the news. How might you use this as a link into the message of the Bible?

6. McClung writes, "People are not merely souls to be won. They are people to be loved and respected" (p. 173). Why is it all too easy to slip into thinking of "souls to be won" as things rather than as people made in God's image?

7. What can we do to not fall into this pattern of thinking?

8. If we don't measure the success of our evangelism by the number of

converts we get, how do we measure it (pp. 176-77)?

9. Look at the list of suggestions for getting started that are found on pages 178-79. What problems would you expect in trying to implement these?

10. What could you do to overcome those problems?

11. What personal barriers do you face in sharing the gospel with your friends? How can these barriers best be overcome?

Fourteen

Overcoming Fear

I ONCE heard a man say, "To love lost souls to me is no chore. My big problem is the man next door."

It certainly is no chore to love people who don't know Christ and live a thousand miles away. It is much easier to do that than to speak up to a classmate, coworker or an obnoxious and critical neighbor.

When it is time to speak up to a person, to lovingly confront him or her with Christ's claim, there is that sinking feeling in the pit of the stomach, that worry about what the friend will think, a feeling of insecurity and uncertainty about what words we will use. Thoughts flow quickly. "Will they mock me? Will they just think I am a fool?"

Proverbs 29:25 warns, "Fear of man will prove to be a snare."

At one time or another, even Billy Graham, like every other Christian, has experienced fear when it comes to personally sharing the gospel.

I know I have. When I was nineteen I went door-to-door with a friend to share the gospel for the first time in my life. I went up to the first door and knocked. When the lady of the house answered, I said very nervously, "Hello, this is my friend, John. My name is Jesus Christ, and we would like to talk to you about Floyd."

Fortunately, the humor of the moment broke the ice, and the lady asked us what we really wanted to talk about. I confessed my nervousness and then told her our purpose was simply to tell people about the joy and forgiveness we had found in Christ. Much to my amazement, she stood in the doorway and listened for quite some time. She was deeply touched by the simple testimony we gave of our relationships with Christ.

Different Kinds of Fear

It might be helpful to examine more carefully the kinds of fear that people experience and why these fears keep people from sharing their faith in Jesus Christ. Danny Lehman, in his great book on personal evangelism, *Bringing 'Em Back Alive,* mentions several different kinds of fear.[1]

The first is the fear of rejection. This is particularly true in our performance-oriented Western world. If we wear the right clothes, say the right things and wear the right cologne, then we will be accepted. We are raised from our earliest moments to look for approval from others. There is a deep fear that people will reject us or think we are crazy if we say the wrong thing or act a bit foolish.

It is helpful to remember that Jesus was "despised and rejected by men" (Is 53:3). There are times when people will reject us because of what we say to them. Perhaps it will be out of misunderstanding or maybe because the Holy Spirit is convicting them of their own sin.

Most people go through a stage where they become very angry and bitter toward Christians because of a deep awareness of their own sinfulness. We must be willing to bear this rejection and to lovingly and graciously continue to be faithful in sharing the gospel of Jesus Christ. If we allow fear of rejection to keep us from speaking up, many who desperately need Christ, and secretly in their hearts want peace and forgiveness, will not find him.

The Bible assures us that "in the fear of the LORD there is strong confidence" (Prov 14:26 NASB). If we put our trust in God, he will give us confidence. He will take the most shy, timid persons and give them the quiet assurance so that they can speak boldly and forcefully of what they believe.

People speak openly about their sexual exploits, their political convictions, their views about philosophy, the weather, sports and every other thing that enters their minds. Why is it that we as Christians do not have the right to express our convictions?

I am not talking about forcing something on other people. There is a difference between experiencing rejection because of the way we say something and because of the message we share. If someone rejects us because we are belligerent or insensitive, then that is our responsibility. But if we simply speak about our beliefs about God, humanity or the nature of sin, and people reject us, then that shows a lack of depth and tolerance on their part. That is their problem, not ours. We must not allow their unwillingness to listen openly to what we have to say keep us from sharing our faith.

I challenge you now, as one who has often failed in this area, to choose to obey the Lord and to use every opportunity possible to speak up regardless of the possibility of rejection.

Fear of losing our reputation is the second kind of fear. As Danny Lehman points out in his book,[2] the best way to deal with the fear of losing our reputation is to give up our reputation! We are to follow the example of the Lord Jesus who gave up his own reputation: "taking the very nature of a servant, being made in human likeness. And being found in appearance as a man, he humbled himself" (Phil 2:7-8).

We must be more concerned about what God thinks of us than what people think. In fact, the big question in life is not, "Can we trust God?" but "Can God trust us?" Will we be faithful and loyal to him in every situation?

There comes a point when we must recognize that these inner fears that we experience can produce sin. If we allow our fears to determine our actions, then we have become a slave to our fears. The Bible says the primary way to deal with fear, as with all sin, is through confession. 1 John 1:9 says, "If we confess our sins, he is faithful and just and will forgive us our sins and purify us from all unrighteousness."

A third kind of fear is the fear of physical harm. I have experienced this walking through the inner city of Amsterdam. Some of our evangelists in Youth With A Mission have spoken of the fear of people reacting physically.

I have had threats against my life, so this is very personal and real to me. I have had to come to the place where I can honestly say to the Lord: "I don't like pain and I don't want to die. I feel that if I face a situation where my life is threatened, I might deny you. But Lord, I trust you. I believe you are able to give me the grace I need when I face that kind of a situation. Therefore, I choose to trust that you are able to help me in any situation I face."

Christians in the early church also faced these kinds of fear. Look at the situation in chapter four in the book of Acts and how those Christians responded to it: "And now, Lord, take note of their threats, and grant that Thy bond-servants may speak Thy word with all confidence. . . . And when they had prayed . . . they were all filled with the Holy Spirit, and *began* to speak the word of God with boldness (Acts 4:29-31 NASB).

The best way to overcome the fear of physical harm is to acknowledge it, confess it, and affirm our trust in the Lord. He is able to give us the grace to face any situation we might find ourselves in. Don't live in such fear of anticipated danger that you miss the joy of God's love right now.

The fourth fear is that of being inadequate. This is the kind of fear that makes us afraid that we will not have the right words to say when we talk to someone, or that they will ask us a question that we will not be able to answer. This is the simplest kind of fear and the easiest to overcome.

Reading books on evangelism (see the further reading section) helps us to overcome this fear. I also encourage you to attend classes on this subject. If you had an inadequacy on the job and you had to overcome it to do your job, then you would most likely enroll in a training course offered for your work. In other words, people take practical steps to get the tools they need to do the job they have to do. It is the same way with evangelism. God can give us the tools we need to do the job. If we will seek him and practically reach out and equip ourselves, then soon our fear will leave.

In fact, as we get experience, we begin to learn that most questions fall into a pattern. We can learn to anticipate them and how to answer them. People's objections to Christianity are often pretty superficial. It will not take you long, through some practical experience, to learn how to deal with them. Besides that, what most people want to hear is your personal testimony. They are impressed with joy, peace and a sense of reality in a person's life. That is the one thing that you have that no one can deny!

God is able to deliver us from all fears. In fact, the Bible says that "perfect love drives out fear" (1 Jn 4:18). One of the greatest ways to overcome fear is by choosing to pray for people and to love them with God's love. A practical way to do this is to take the names of three non-Christians and begin to pray for them on a regular basis. Ask the Lord to give you thoughts on how to pray for them and how to love them in a practical manner.

Pray that they will have understanding of the gospel. Pray that God will lead them to Christian friends whom they will be able to listen to. Pray that they will be able to find literature that will speak to them about their needs for God. Pray that they will hear the gospel through the media. Pray that they will come to a place physically and emotionally where they will cry out to God in their hearts.

Receive God's love for these individuals by faith. It is an act of faith, not feeling, to love people, especially when they are difficult to love. Ask God to fill your heart with his love for them. He will gladly do it. People will begin to see the difference in you. You can also ask God to give you inspiration and thoughts about how you can express that love to people in a practical way.

Perfect love, God's love, does drive out our fear. If we stop thinking about ourselves, and we start thinking about others, effective evangelism will begin!

Questions for Individuals or Groups

1. What fears do you have about talking to people about Jesus?

2. Why is fear of what other people will think of us so common when we think about doing evangelism (pp. 182-83)?

3. What can help us overcome such fears?

4. Have you personally or have you known people who were threatened physically for trying to witness (pp. 184-85)? Describe the situation.

5. How do you think we should respond to such situations?

6. The last fear the author mentions is that of feeling inadequately prepared to explain the message of salvation or to answer questions about it that people might have (pp. 185-86). Where is your preparation strong, and where could it be improved?

7. What steps could you take to be better prepared?

8. How can love cast out fear as you consider talking to others about Jesus?

Notes

[1]Danny Lehman, *Bringing 'Em Back Alive*. Chicago, Ill.: Whitaker House, 1987.

[2]Ibid.

Afterword

Being committed to Jesus as Lord does not mean we will never fail. There will be times of discouragement and struggle. When such times arise in our lives, we must remember that God is committed to us far more than we will ever be committed to him.

Paul tells us, "There is now no condemnation for those who are in Christ Jesus, because through Christ Jesus the law of the Spirit of life set me free from the law of sin and death. For what the law was powerless to do in that it was weakened by the sinful nature, God did by sending his own Son in the likeness of sinful man to be a sin offering. And so he condemned sin in sinful man, in order that the righteous requirements of the law might be fully met in us, who do not live according to the sinful nature but according to the Spirit" (Rom 8:1-4). We do not live under condemnation. We are set free by what Christ has done to live in and through the Spirit.

What does this life look like? Jesus said, "I have come that they may have life, and have it to the full" (Jn 10:10). This abundant life is what God desires for us and has made possible for us. I have come to believe and know from experience this freedom and joy and power. As I've said before, this doesn't mean we will never sin or never have problems in our lives. But because God is on our side, because he has given us grace through his Son, we can experience victory. God has done it. Let us rejoice in it.

Further Reading on Evangelism

Tom Eisenman, *Everyday Evangelism,* Downers Grove, Ill.: Inter-Varsity Press, 1987.

Danny Lehman, *Bringing 'Em Back Alive,* Chicago, Ill.: Whitaker House, 1987.

C. S. Lewis, *Mere Christianity,* 1952. *Miracles,* 1947. *The Problem of Pain,* 1940. All now published as Fount Paperbacks.

Floyd McClung, Jr., *The Father Heart of God,* Kingsway, 1985.

Josh McDowell, *Evidence That Demands a Verdict,* San Bernardino, Calif.: Here's Life Publishers, 1979. *More Evidence That Demands a Verdict,* San Bernardino, Calif.: Here's Life Publishers, 1981.

Rebecca Manley Pippert, *Out of the Saltshaker & Into the World,* InterVarsity Press, 1980.

Don Richardson, *Eternity in Their Hearts,* Ventura, Calif.: Regal, 1975. *Peace Child,* Ventura, Calif.: Regal, 1984.

Bilas Sheikh, *I Dared to Call Him Father,* Send the Light, 1979.

Floyd and Sally McClung work with Youth With A Mission in Amsterdam, Holland. For more information about their work write to their U.S. office:

Youth With A Mission
4931 Lori Ann
Irvine, CA 92714